Dowsing

for health

tuning in to the
earth's energy for
personal development
and wellbeing

Dowsing

for health

dr patrick macmanaway

This book is dedicated with love and admiration to my parents, Bruce and Patricia MacManaway, whose vision and integrity served the unqualified return of the spirit of healing and dowsing to the community.

First published in 2001 by Lorenz Books

© 2001 Anness Publishing Limited

Lorenz Books is an imprint of
Anness Publishing Limited, Hermes House
88-89 Blackfriars Road, London SE1 8HA

Published in the USA by Lorenz Books,
Anness Publishing Inc., 27 West 20th Street,New York, NY 10011

www.lorenzbooks.com

This edition distributed in Canada by
Raincoast Books, 9050 Shaughnessy Street
Vancouver British Columbia V6P 6E5

A CIP catalogue record for this book is available from the British Library

Publisher: **Joanna Lorenz**
Managing Editor: **Helen Sudell**
Project Editors: **Emma Gray and Debra Mayhew**
Jacket and Style Designer: **Lisa Tai**
Page Designer: **Jane Coney**
Photography: **Don Last**
Production Controller: **Don Campaniello**
Editorial Reader: **Diane Ashmore**
Illustrators: **David Cook and Ben Cracknell**

10 9 8 7 6 5 4 3 2

Publisher's note: The reader should not regard the recommendations, ideas and techniques expressed and described in this book as substitutes for the advice of a qualified medical practitioner or other qualified professional. Any use to which the recommendations, ideas and techniques are put is at the reader's sole discretion and risk.

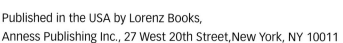

Contents

Introduction 6

chapter 1

Doorway to Wholeness 8

chapter 2

Pathway to Health 22

chapter 3

Vital Healing 40

chapter 4

Earth Energies 54

chapter 5

Landscape Synergy 70

chapter 6

Dowsing Deeper 84

Index, Useful Addresses
and Acknowledgements 96

introduction

The ability to dowse is a simple and natural gift of the human spirit, present in each one of us from birth. It is a method for bringing our awake, alert, rational consciousness into direct communication and dialogue with our intuition and inner wisdom.

When exploring and interpreting the world around us, we depend to a great extent on our five "primary" senses – touch, taste, smell, hearing and sight. It is an often mentioned paradox that while we are so dependent on their information, the nature of their respective sensory organs is to limit and filter to a manageable amount what would otherwise be an overwhelming quantity of sensory stimulation. For example, the eyes respond only to the range of electromagnetic frequencies that for us is the "visual spectrum" – the rainbow palette that colours and defines the world and all that is in it. Yet this visual spectrum is but a wafer-thin band of a vast range of frequencies reaching far above and below the ability of our human senses to perceive.

Intuition is sometimes described as the "sixth sense", and although it remains the least understood of the senses, it is perhaps the most powerful and in some respects the most truly primary sense of all. One of the central mysteries of life is the interconnectedness of all things. Through our intuition, we are able to perceive and experience this interconnectedness, and gather virtually unlimited information far beyond the reach of the other senses. The imagination is the sensory organ of the intuition and while the rich textures of the imagination can guide and inspire us in a general way, to interpret intuitive information in a specific and detailed fashion requires focus and discipline.

Dowsing is just such a disciplined focus, bridging the gap between rational and intuitive, and giving us potentially unlimited access to information about the world of which we are an integral part.

Using dowsing to explore and enhance our health is one of the most practical and affirming uses of this simple and natural miracle of human consciousness.

Doorway to Wholeness

The breeze at dawn has secrets to tell you.

Don't go back to sleep.

You must ask for what you really want.

Don't go back to sleep.

People are going back and forth across the doorsill

where the two worlds touch.

The door is round and open.

Don't go back to sleep.

Rumi (1207–1273)

Health and wholeness

This book is an invitation to explore a uniquely personal and radically powerful path to extraordinary health. It will guide you in opening and cultivating a dialogue with your inner self – your wisdom self. This part of you knows what your body needs to be healthy, it knows what your mind needs for stimulation and satisfaction, and it knows what your spirit needs for the celebration of its self-expression and the fulfilment of its purpose on the planet.

the nature of health

What is health, and what does it mean to be healthy? We may often think and talk about health, both our own and that of other people, but what do we really mean by the term? Often when we talk about health we are referring to how well our body is functioning for us, and think of health in physical terms. People also speak about their health in feeling terms, and we may ask someone how they are feeling as a way of inquiring after their health. We might hear "I'm feeling fine" or "I'm not feeling very good today", and understand that our emotional state also plays a part in our concept of health.

We use the word "health" in many different ways and to communicate somewhat different things, depending on the context and circumstances.

The World Health Organization defines it like this: "Health is a state of complete physical, mental, and social wellbeing and not merely the absence of disease or infirmity." This is a very helpful definition. It guides us to assess health in positive terms of wellbeing rather than in terms of impairment, and to include in our health assessment the nature and quality of our relationships, including our role as members of a community.

The word "health" comes from the same root as the word "whole", and this may be a key to understanding its more comprehensive meaning. Assessing health in terms of how far or fast we can run, how attractive we think we are, or how often or seldom we experience physical or emotional discomfort, leads us to a very limited sense of ourselves and our lives. Turning our attention towards how whole our lives can be and how complete and integrated we can become as human beings, both in relation to ourselves and to our community, leads us in an altogether more powerful, liberating, and genuinely interesting direction.

Seen in this context, health is perhaps not definable as an externally measured state but as a life fully experienced and lived.

the holistic paradigm

Increasingly, many of us are learning to assess health not only in terms of our minds and our bodies, but also to include the element of spirit.

"Spirit", rather like "health", is a word that we all define a little differently, and this similarly tells us something important – it is something whose nature is unique and quite individual. We might agree however, that it has to do with the deepest and truest part of ourselves, our essence, or "inner self", related to, but different from our physical body and our thoughts.

The holistic paradigm is one in which every part of a human being – body, mind and spirit – is considered. Furthermore, it is understood that these three elements are interwoven, interdependent, and reflective of each other.

In terms of health, this means that any physical imbalance is also associated with a related disturbance in the mind and spirit,

◁ **Reading a book can offer an enlightening source of personal insights.**

▽ **Health unfolds in our lives as a consequence of the healthy choices we take.**

and that for complete physical healing to occur, balance must be restored in all three dimensions of our being.

Discussing spirit in the context of health can make some of us feel uncomfortable. An acceptance of the reality of spirit and its relationship with the mind and body is as old at least as oral history, and has been forgotten only relatively recently as we have become increasingly fascinated by the development of science and new material technology. For many of us, matters of the spirit seem abstract and removed from our lives, and following a spiritual path seems incompatible with the pressures of modern life. However, by allowing our fears and concerns to dominate us, we may be missing an important point and one that could be highly rewarding and enriching.

Let us consider a paradox: it could be that we are not so much human beings who may choose to walk a spiritual path, but rather spiritual beings who have chosen to walk a human path. If this proposition is true, then it can change how we live our lives and our attitude to the world. From this perspective, health may be seen as the acceptance and expression of our uniqueness, allowing our true self to be totally present and fully engaged and allowing us to experience our lives as fully as we would wish.

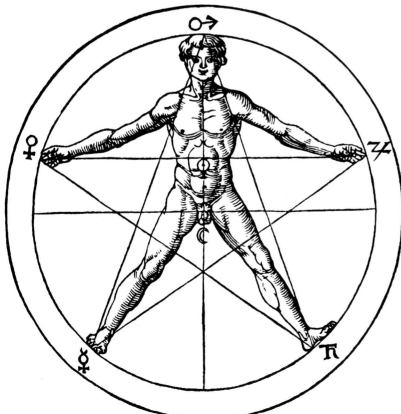

△ Allowing space and time in our lives to listen to the small, still voice within, in whatever way feels most natural and comfortable, begins the process of aligning body, mind and spirit.

◁ The study of the anatomy and functions of the human spirit have traditionally been an integral part of natural science, and is essential to a complete understanding of health.

Part of the process of reaching a state of greater self-acceptance and self-expression is learning to trust the inner self, and to receive its wisdom. This wise self knows who we are and what we need and will bring us towards ever greater experiences of joy and peace. This joy and peace is the reality of the balanced interaction between body, mind and spirit.

This spirit self has a small, still voice. One of the ways that we can learn to listen closely to it is by learning how to dowse.

A doorway to the inner world

Dowsing is a simple and natural process, and is a universal human ability. It bridges the rational, intellectual part of ourselves with the intuitive, wise part of ourselves. It is like a doorway between the mind and spirit, using our body as the threshold. Both an art and a science, dowsing is a holistic discipline, teaching us to develop and use our intellect and intuition together, and to engage in matters of concern with a sincere but unattached focus. The more respect that we bring to our dowsing, the more reliable it will be.

Studies monitoring the brainwaves that are generated by dowsers reveal a range of frequencies and a balance between the left and right hemispheres of the brain which is comparable with those of long-term meditators and yogis. This is indicative of both a balanced and an expanded sensory perception that is accessed through dowsing, and affirms it as an authentic method to gently align body, mind and spirit.

◁ **The uses of dowsing are limited only by our imagination. This woodcut shows the use of dowsing to locate and extract mineral ore, a practice that continues to the present day.**

basic principles of dowsing

The process of dowsing involves asking a question and is generally used to discover information that we either cannot get in any other way or that we do not have quick or easy access to. A genuine need to know the answer is a key factor for dowsing to work well, along with "unattached curiosity". This means having a calm and open mind as to what the answer will be. If we are too emotionally "attached" to a particular outcome, this can negatively influence our dowsing abilities. Attaining this state of unattached curiosity is one of the most important and valuable quests.

When we pose a dowsing question, we are asking with the rational, intellectual, thinking part of our mind. Then, having asked the question, we wait, patiently and with engaged but unattached curiosity, for the answer to come back to us. This is a little like watching for the results of an internet search, or for the weather to change, there is little we can do to influence the outcome, except to ask the most salient question.

The answer comes back to us almost immediately, in the form of a symbolic movement or change of movement in the tool that we are dowsing with. This is the voice of our intuition, of our inner or spirit self, using our dowsing tool as a mouthpiece.

◁ **There are many doors to the inner world, and many ways of passing through them. Dowsing is one way to cross the threshold.**

intellect and intuition

Many people are highly intuitive and have had experiences of surrendering to and being completely overtaken by their intuition, often in tremendously creative and artistically expressive ways. Compared with this, dowsing seems very tame! Mostly in dowsing we allow our intuition only to say "Yes" or "No" and so it may be difficult to imagine how we can expect intuitive expression with such simple answers.

This is where a balanced and common-sense attitude is needed. To dowse well, we must ask the right questions, and in doing so we learn to focus our mind on asking questions that are appropriate and timely. It is about bringing our intellect into alignment with the needs and concerns of our spirit. This alignment allows many blessings and good things to enter our lives in many different areas, quite unexpectedly.

When we are dowsing, we need to remain alert and aware of ourselves, exercising reason and discrimination. It is not about completely surrendering ourselves to intuition and irrational forces. This means that dowsing can be integrated into every part of our lives without disruption or disturbance and help us towards an experience of increasing wholeness rather than one of chaos and disintegration.

how dowsing works

Dowsing works very simply. We ask a clear and unambiguous question in our mind, to which the answer can only be "Yes" or "No". Having asked the question, we allow the answer to come back to us from our inner self, using a predetermined code to interpret the movements of the dowsing tool to indicate whether it is a positive or a negative response.

Dowsing is a gateway to the intuition, bridging the gap between the mind and spirit.

DOWSING TOOLS

The most familiar tools that dowsers use nowadays are the pendulum, the L-rod, the Y-rod or forked stick, the bobber and, more recently, the aurameter. The movement of the dowsing tool or instrument is caused by the movement of the dowser's muscles. However, for the dowser the experience is that the tool is moving by itself. This is because the action is not voluntary or intended but occurs involuntarily, in the same way as a yawn, a laugh, a heartbeat or a breath. The dowsing movement occurs completely naturally without our needing to make it happen.

▷ **The simple pendulum is universally popular, versatile and convenient. It can be anything from a ring or a crystal weight on a thread. Although often very personalized, anything that swings freely will serve as an effective pendulum.**

◁ **L-rods are excellent field-tools, and are particularly useful for searching and locating in dowsing tasks. They can be quickly and inexpensively made by bending any piece of wire to form a right-angle, with the arm longer than the handle.**

▷ **The bobber or wand is a traditional dowsing tool, and can be made by cutting a springy branch and holding its narrow end, so that it can easily bounce or bob. Metal bobbers can also be bought and used in the same way and are just as effective.**

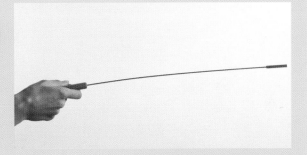

◁ **The Y-rod or V-rod is a time-honoured and still popular dowsing tool, much favoured by water and mineral dowsers. Traditionally it is cut from a tree, often hazel, willow or apple, but modern plastics also work just as well.**

▷ **Many custom-made and sophisticated dowsing tools are also available. This aurameter combines high-tensile wire with a spring-swivel in the handle to create a delightfully sensitive and highly visual dowsing tool.**

The journey begins

When learning to dowse, a pendulum is an excellent tool for the beginner, and for many remains forever the tool of choice. The pendulum is perhaps the most convenient as well as the most versatile of dowsing tools. It is easily carried about in a pocket, can be worn as jewellery or can be made spontaneously from almost anything to hand.

choosing a pendulum

To make a pendulum suitable for dowsing, we need something that can be suspended from a thread, chain, piece of string or other cord. Ideally a pendulum is symmetrical and attached to its cord centrally, so that it can swing perfectly freely in any direction. If this does not happen, and it has any tendency to an asymmetrical or unbalanced motion, this can compromise its use.

In truth, almost anything that swings freely can be used as a pendulum. This can include a ring suspended on a piece of thread or hair, a hexagonal nut tied to a piece of string, or even keys on a chain can be used as a pendulum. Take a look around and you'll see many possibilities for creating unique and surprising pendulums! The only important thing about choosing a pendulum is that it swings freely and easily.

After a while, however, most dowsers find a pendulum that "feels right" in their hand and which they keep with them and use consistently when dowsing. Much like an artist's favourite paintbrush or maybe a carpenter's best tool, dowsers tend to develop a familiarity and ease with a particular weight and balance in their hand, and often develop a preference for a pendulum made from one particular material. Many pendulums are made from wood, others from polished stones or crystals, sometimes plastics, and many from metals of various kinds. The choice is really up to you. Don't get too attached to your pendulum, however, remember that dowsing is an inner process, and that your pendulum is simply a tool for discovering wisdom and not the source of it.

Dowsing preparation

Although it's not strictly necessary to sit or stand in a special way, a good posture helps to relax the body and keep the mind alert. Either sit or stand with your feet firmly and evenly balanced on the floor, about shoulder-width apart, and hold your spine erect.

▷ **1** Hold the cord of your pendulum between the thumb and forefinger of your dominant hand (that means the right hand for right-handed people and the left hand for left-handed people) with the tips of the thumb and forefinger pointing downwards to allow the pendulum to swing freely. The greater the distance between your fingers and the pendulum, the longer and slower the pendulum will move. In contrast, if you hold the pendulum on a very short cord, it will swing about in a quick, lively fashion. There is no right or wrong length, but a distance of approximately 5–8 cm (2–3 in) generally gives a nice responsive action.

▽ **2** Hold your pendulum centrally between and a little above the height of your knees and start it swinging in a to-and-fro motion towards and away from you. This is the neutral or search position, and means "I am ready to start dowsing".

Basic dowsing responses

What we need to establish next are the pendulum motions that will mean "Yes" and "No" for you. These vary from person to person and the key is knowing what your personal dowsing responses are.

▷ **1** With your pendulum swinging back and forth, move your hand over until your pendulum is swinging over your dominant-side knee (right side for right-handers, left side for left-handers) and state clearly and simply in your mind "Please show me my 'Yes' response".

2 Pay close attention to what the pendulum does. It may change its back and forth swing to a clockwise or anti-clockwise motion, it may alter the direction of its swing from towards and away from you to a diagonal swing or even a side-to-side swing, or it might stop swinging altogether. Whatever it does, this will now be your signal for "Yes".

◁ **3** Now take your pendulum back to its neutral swing between your knees, and this time move your hand over until your pendulum is swinging over your non-dominant side knee and state clearly and simply in your mind "Please show me my 'No' response".

4 Closely observe what your pendulum does – it should change its swing to something clearly different from either your "Neutral" or "Yes" response. This new response is your signal for "No".

5 Repeat the exercise several times to become confident and familiar with your responses, taking your pendulum between the "Neutral", "Yes" and "No" positions and allowing the responses to develop fully over each knee.

creating your own signals

If you find that your dowsing responses are not working or don't come easily, don't worry. Many of us have a bit of difficulty in getting dowsing to work when we first start. We are trying to establish a connection with a part of ourselves that may have been dormant for quite a long time, so we can afford to be patient and take the time to wake it up slowly and gently.

The dowsing responses you get are the signals between your intellect and your intuition, and if the intuition does not seem to readily or clearly volunteer a signal for "Yes" and "No", we can invite our intellect to choose one.

To find your "Yes" response, hold the pendulum over your dominant knee and deliberately set it into a new motion which you choose to be your "Yes" signal and affirm clearly in your mind "This is my signal for 'Yes'".

Choosing a different signal, repeat over the non-dominant knee to establish your "No" response, affirming clearly in your mind "This is my signal for 'No'".

Once you have established your chosen "Yes" and "No" signals, make your pendulum move between the neutral and the "Yes/No" positions several times to develop confidence and familiarity with each response. After a short period of time your chosen responses will become completely automatic and spontaneous and you will be able to use your dowsing with confidence.

PENDULUM RESPONSES

The diagrams on the right show classic pendulum dowsing responses. You will see the introductory neutral which is a "towards and away from you" swing, and the "clockwise for 'Yes'" and "anti-clockwise for 'No'" responses. While by no means universal, many dowsers find that these or a version of these, are the responses that their pendulum gives them when dowsing. Dowsing responses are a very individual and personal thing however, and you need not worry whether yours are the same as, or different from anyone else's. It only matters that they feel natural and right for you, and that you know which is which.

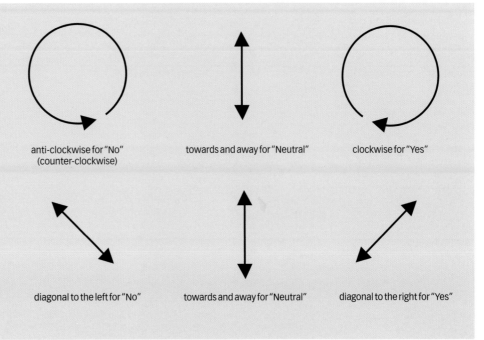

anti-clockwise for "No"
(counter-clockwise)

towards and away for "Neutral"

clockwise for "Yes"

diagonal to the left for "No"

towards and away for "Neutral"

diagonal to the right for "Yes"

Dowsing exercises

Having established our pendulum's signals for "Yes" and "No", we have opened the doorway for a dialogue that can allow us to follow many paths and to apply dowsing usefully in our and even other peoples lives. To begin with however, some fun but simple exercises will allow us to practise crossing backwards and forwards between our rational intellect and intuition, getting swift, clear dowsing responses and learning to keep an open mind, in a state of engaged non-attachment.

cup and ball exercise

Ideally, practice exercises in dowsing should be fun and engaging. They should involve our asking questions to which the answer can only be "Yes" or "No", any ambiguity will make this exercise very difficult. Also, we should be able to get instant feedback on whether our dowsing was correct or not. Simple hiding games such as hiding a ball under a cup and dowsing to find its position, are easy to set up and fun to do by yourself or with a friend.

△ **The innocent nature of hide and seek games is ideal for engaging both intellect and intuition.**

◁ **Set up practice exercises so that a full and correct answer is either yes or no, and where feedback is instant.**

playing cards exercise

A slightly more complex and longer exercise can be done with playing cards. Take an ordinary pack of playing cards and remove the jokers. Lie the pack face-down in front of you. We will begin by identifying whether the top card belongs to one of the black suits (clubs and spades) or to one of the red suits (diamonds and hearts).

Sitting comfortably, with your spine erect and your body relaxed, focus on the card at the top of the pile. You may wish to rest a finger on it to help you focus more completely, or even take it off the pack and place it face down on the table on its own. Start your pendulum in its to-and-fro, neutral swing, and ask clearly in your mind: "Does this card belong to one of the black suits?"

Hold the question in your mind without worrying whether the card is black or red, and observe as your pendulum changes its motion from the to-and-fro of the neutral swing to either your "Yes" or "No" response.

Once you have your response – in this case a "Yes" would indicate a black card and a "No" would indicate a red card – turn the card over and see whether your dowsing was correct. It was? Congratulations! It wasn't? Not to worry, try again.

Work your way gradually through the whole pack. As you go, allow your mind to become increasingly patient and relaxed: stay alert, but let go of all attachment to which colour the card will be or even to whether or not your dowsing is accurate. Paradoxically, greater accuracy comes as we let go of our need to control the outcome and of our investment in being right or wrong.

As you go through the pack, put the cards that you dowsed correctly in one pile and the cards that you dowsed incorrectly in another. This will give you a measure of your success and allow you to monitor your progress.

You will probably find that the state of open-minded, engaged non-attachment is easiest to achieve when you are alone, at least to begin with, and that consistent accuracy becomes harder in the presence of onlookers who you may wish to convince or impress. Don't stake your reputation on your dowsing this early in your career.

refining your skill

If you enjoyed the card-dowsing exercise, you can take it a step further, and dowse each card to find out exactly which member of the pack it is. In order to do this, we have to stay with questions to which the whole and complete answer is an unambiguous "Yes" or "No". By asking carefully, we can narrow the possibilities down by half each time.

Start by asking if the card is black. Let's assume the answer is "Yes". Next ask if it is a member of the suit of clubs – let's say the answer now is a "No". With only two

▷ **Although it is often easier to focus on our dowsing when we are alone and undistracted, it can be fun, supportive and encouraging to share our exploration of dowsing with friends. It is also very helpful to practice with skilled and experienced dowsers.**

▷ **The great number of possibilities offered by a pack of cards helps us to learn to keep dowsing question-asking clear, efficient and unambiguous.**

questions, we have found that the card is a member of the suit of spades. But which one is it?

A good question will reduce our options by half. "Is this card higher than a seven?" (You need to decide whether you are counting aces high or low). Let's assume the answer is "Yes" this time.

Divide the possibilities in half again: "Is this a court-card? We get the answer "No". At this point, we have only three options: it is either the eight, nine or ten of spades. Once you have narrowed the possibilities down this far, it is easy to simply ask which number it is, one by one: "Is this card the eight of spades?" "No". "Is this card the nine of spades?" "Yes." Now turn the card over and see if your dowsing was accurate.

You may find that this is an easy exercise and that you get consistently accurate answers. If not, please don't be discouraged. Some of the very best dowsers have had to be patient in the beginning to cultivate consistently accurate responses. Also, some exercises appeal and engage us more than others, and it will be easiest to get good

dowsing responses from an exercise that captures your attention and invites your curiosity. You could try a similar but simplified version of number dowsing using a set of dominoes.

When creating dowsing exercises, we are only limited by our imagination. Whichever ones you try, remember to keep them simple and fun, to be sure that the correct response can only be a "Yes/No" answer, and that you can get instant feedback.

Talking more with your pendulum

Now that we have gained some basic skill with our pendulum, we can develop our dowsing vocabulary a little further to prepare us for working in real life situations.

For the beginner, the response from the pendulum is the most mysterious and unfamiliar part of dowsing. After a little practice however, the movements of the pendulum or other dowsing tool become perfectly automatic and natural, and then the main task of dowsing becomes one of asking clear, concise, and unambiguous questions.

Ideally, a dowsing question should always be framed in such a way that either "Yes" or "No" is a complete and accurate response. Sometimes this is hard to do – particularly when we are dowsing about topic areas where we are relatively ignorant. If dowsing to identify a mechanical problem in our car, for example, those of us with expert mechanical knowledge will be able to ask specific, focused and relevant questions. Others may have a little knowledge, and ask questions that they think are focused and precise, but which in fact are ambiguous and could be misleading if answered, "Yes" or "No".

Recognizing the limits of our intellectual knowledge and understanding is important and even humbling at times. It is often best to start our inquiry from absolute basics, with a beginner's mind, thereby minimizing or avoiding the pitfalls of our assumptions.

dowsing responses

In addition to asking careful questions, however, we can also get a helpful guiding nudge from our intuition to steer us back on track when we start to stray. This is made possible by three additional dowsing responses: "Yes, but ...", "No, but ..." and "Unanswerable question". The former two signals are of immense help in guiding us to ask more complete and precise questions, and can save us from getting hopelessly misled, while the latter can be particularly helpful when we are pursuing a misleading path. When you get one of these responses, it alerts you to the fact that your question cannot be completely or accurately answered, or that you are going in the wrong direction.

As before, sit comfortably and relaxed with your spine erect and your feet shoulder-width

Let your imagination roam free and the realms of your knowledge will stretch towards infinity

apart on the floor. Hold your pendulum in the search position and establish your to-and-fro neutral swing. Move your pendulum over your dominant-side knee and let it develop into its full "Yes" signal.

Now, bring it back one-third of the way towards the midline, neutral position, and as you do so, ask clearly in your mind to be shown your "Yes, but ..." signal. This may be a half-developed "Yes" signal – which may be an almost lazy "sort of yes" answer, or it may be a new direction of swing from any of your previous responses.

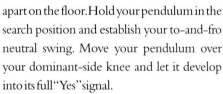

△ In areas where we lack expert knowledge, a return to beginners' state of mind helps us to frame basic and relevant questions.

◁ Crystal pendulums are easy to find and are beautiful objects to work with.

OTHER BASIC PENDULUM RESPONSES

Very often if a "Yes" is a fully developed circular motion, either clockwise or anti-clockwise, the "Yes, but ..." will be an ellipse in the same direction, the degree of certainty being expressed by the fullness of the circle that develops. Similarly if your "Yes" signal is a diagonal swing, for example half-left to half-right, the "Yes, but ..." may be an incompletely developed diagonal, say quarter-left to quarter-right. "No" responses would then be the opposite. "Unanswerable question" is typically marked by a side-to-side swing.

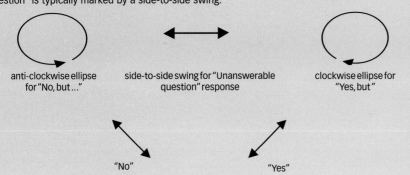

anti-clockwise ellipse for "No, but ..."

side-to-side swing for "Unanswerable question" response

clockwise ellipse for "Yes, but"

"No"

"Yes"

△ **When learning to dowse, keep your fingers pointed downwards to allow the pendulum to swing freely.**

Bring your pendulum back to your midline neutral position and swing, and then go over your non-dominant knee and let it develop its normal "No" response. Now bring it back one-third of the way towards the midline and ask clearly in your mind to be shown your "No, but ..." signal.

Finally, go back to your neutral swing, and ask clearly in your mind to be shown your "Unanswerable question" response. Often this response is a side-to-side swing, although it may be anything, provided it is clear and different from your other responses. You do not need to move your pendulum for this signal – it will develop in the midline.

As with your original establishment of the "Yes" and "No" signals, if your pendulum does not spontaneously offer you these three signals, you can choose yourself what they will be and swing the pendulum in the "Yes, but ...", "No, but ..." and "Unanswerable question" motions of your choice while affirming: "This is my signal for 'Yes, but ...'" and so forth. You can do this in conjunction with the dowsing response chart.

Whether they come to you spontaneously or by your active choice, repeatedly practise the different responses in their appropriate positions until they feel automatic and entirely natural.

response reversal

Sometimes, when we are tired, or under considerable stress, or if we are dowsing for something which is close to us emotionally, our dowsing responses may become reversed, so that our normal "Yes" becomes our "No" and our normal "No" becomes our "Yes". This does not seem to affect all dowsers equally. Some dowsers never experience this phenomenon at all. Others experience it intermittently, particularly when they are first learning.

The wisest strategy is to check your "Yes/No" signal each time you begin to dowse. Then you can be sure that you and your pendulum are speaking the same language.

△ **To use a dowsing chart hold the pendulum over the base of the chart and start with your neutral swing on the centre line. Ask your question and allow the pendulum to point towards a response.**

RESPONSE EXERCISE CHART

Now you have learned all of the responses you will need to begin working with your pendulum. You can practise all of them using an enlarged version of the dowsing chart shown below to help you. Simply hold your pendulum above each section and the pendulum response should correspond with the movements you have just worked out.

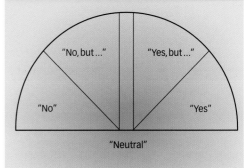

"No, but ..."

"Yes, but ..."

"No"

"Yes"

"Neutral"

It's all in the state of the mind

Once we have become clear about our responses and familiar with the use of the pendulum, we can start to use dowsing on a regular basis in our everyday life. Through much of this book we will be learning ways to use dowsing for enhancing our health and wellbeing and for making increasingly healthy choices in our lives.

Part of integrating dowsing into our lives is to allow it to be a straightforward, commonplace and matter-of-fact activity. Respect your dowsing – you are in dialogue with your spirit – and use it for issues of appropriate and genuine need. It can be helpful to approach your dowsing as though you were asking the advice of someone you love and respect, such as a relative or close friend, or else of a wise and learned sage.

the dowsing sequence

There is a sequence which we follow when dowsing. It has a beginning, a middle and an end.

We begin by clearing our mind of clutter, busyness and preconceptions, and centre ourselves in an alert but peaceful way in our body. How this is done is very individual,

◁ **Find a way that feels natural to clear your mind and centre yourself peacefully in your body before you start to dowse. An alert and engaged, but unattached, state of mind helps us to do our best dowsing.**

and you will discover what works best for you. Avoid dowsing when you are tired or upset as it is difficult to be clear and focused during these times.

Sit or stand quietly for a minute or two and start to become aware of your breathing.

Visualize yourself in a column of golden light, radiating to you from the Divine, the source of universal love. This will enhance and balance the body-mind-spirit connection.

Offer a prayer that your dowsing will be for the greatest good of all beings, or ask for help and guidance from a particular spiritual source. Stay with what feels right to you, and be sure that you are centred in your heart.

Once we are clear, centred and connected, our dowsing can begin.

Sitting or standing comfortably and relaxed, set your pendulum into its neutral swing, and check your "Yes" response. (Do this over your dominant knee, as before.)

Next, state clearly in your mind the overall topic or area of concern that you wish to dowse about. This helps us to "tune in".

Having tuned in, we now ask of our dowsing: "Is it timely and appropriate for me to dowse about this?"

If our dowsing tells us "No", it is not timely and appropriate, then give thanks to your spirit for guiding you, and leave dowsing on that topic for another time. If your answer is "Yes", then you can proceed.

ENGAGED NON-ATTACHMENT

While we are dowsing, we are in a state of engaged non-attachment. This becomes easier the longer we dowse and become familiar with the state. It is important because we can otherwise influence the result of our dowsing by our mind wishing that the response will be either "Yes" or "No".

When we are first learning to dowse (or even when we are experienced) two things can be helpful in engaging the mind so that it does not distort or influence the outcome: continuing to repeat the question that we have asked until our dowsing response is fully established and engaging the mind in child-like curiosity and wonder at what the pendulum is going to do after we have asked our question.

TIMELY AND APPROPRIATE

There are cycles of time which unfold at their own speed, and sometimes answers are not available until their unfolding is complete. Also, there is some information that it may not be appropriate for us to know. Sometimes we have to wait for further pieces of the jigsaw of our life or someone else's life to have been put into place, revealing the emerging pattern of wholeness. A healthy respect for what is timely and appropriate and a philosophical acceptance of "what is" goes a long way towards making a good dowser.

We have now arrived at the middle of our dowsing sequence. During this, we may ask as many questions as we need of our dowsing to discover all the information that can help us on this topic. Try to ask questions that will be fully answered by "Yes" or "No", and pay attention and rethink if you get "Yes, but …", "No, but …" or "Unanswerable question".

Consider the kind of questions you might ask before accepting a job offer.

"Do I have the necessary skills to perform well at this job? Will this job really allow me to express my creativity in the way that I desire? Is the office that I will be working in a healthy environment for me to be in? Is it in the greatest overall good for me and my family for me to accept this job offer?"

When we think we are finished dowsing it is wise to ask: "Is there anything else that I need to know about this now?"

It is also a good idea to make sure that we aren't ending with any misconceptions. State clearly in your mind the key information and conclusions, and then ask: "Is this the truth?"

Finally, to end the dowsing sequence, we can give thanks for the information and guidance received.

▽ **Dowsing blind helps us to ask questions that we are emotionally attached to without compromising our dowsing**.

blind dowsing

Sometimes, we encounter a situation where dowsing would be of benefit but where we are so involved that we cannot be entirely sure that our hopes or fears will not influence the outcome. One technique that we can use at such a time is to dowse "blind". This means that you dowse without knowing what question you are asking. Here's how to do it.

Write your questions on the subject down on separate, but identical pieces of paper. As well as the questions which you want to dowse, you can also write some simple, factual "control" questions to which you already know the answer, such as "Is today Tuesday? Is my name …?" These will help you to check the accuracy of your dowsing, which may be compromised if you are tired or upset. Turn the pieces of paper face-down and shuffle them until you do not know which is which.

Dowse over the papers one by one asking: "What is the answer to the question on this piece of paper?" Make a pile of "Yes" responses and another pile of "No" responses.

Once you have dowsed them all, turn the papers over. The accuracy of your dowsing over the control questions will guide you in interpreting the answers to your concerns.

If your dowsing is inaccurate, you might ask someone less involved to dowse for you (if it is important, you can also have them dowse blind to check their accuracy).

△ **Finding practical uses for our dowsing in everyday life helps us to integrate body, mind and spirit.**

integrating dowsing into life

Start looking for ways to use your dowsing every day, particularly in situations where you can quickly check your accuracy. Keeping a pendulum by the telephone and dowsing to see if the person who you want to speak to is there before you call can be fun. If the answer is "Yes, but …", then maybe they are screening their calls.

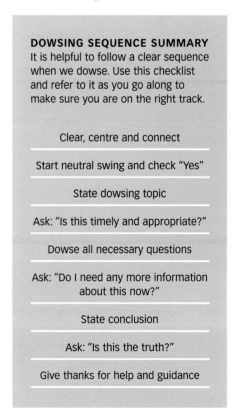

DOWSING SEQUENCE SUMMARY
It is helpful to follow a clear sequence when we dowse. Use this checklist and refer to it as you go along to make sure you are on the right track.

Clear, centre and connect

Start neutral swing and check "Yes"

State dowsing topic

Ask: "Is this timely and appropriate?"

Dowse all necessary questions

Ask: "Do I need any more information about this now?"

State conclusion

Ask: "Is this the truth?"

Give thanks for help and guidance

Pathway to Health

Truth is within ourselves, it takes no rise

From outward things, whate'er you may believe

There is an inner centre in us all

Where truth abides in fullness; and around

Wall upon wall the gross flesh hems it in

That perfect clear perception which is Truth.

A baffling and perverting carnal mesh

Binds all and makes all error, but to know

Rather consists in finding out a way

For the imprisoned splendour to escape

Than in achieving entry for a light

Supposed to be without.

Robert Browning (1812–1889)

Finding true health

Dowsing for information and guidance around our health is one of its most valuable uses, and also one of the best ways to build up dowsing experience and confidence. It is an area of dowsing in which the need is genuine and life affirming, and where the feedback is direct and personally experienced.

Whether dowsing to help us recover from an illness or to enhance our overall wellbeing, the process of bringing focused attention to our health and of integrating our thoughts and activities with the new information and wisdom from our spirit brings into play a powerful alignment of psychic, mental and physical energies. A spiritual law says that whatever we give our energy or attention to is both magnified and attracted to us. Therefore by actively seeking health, we attract it to us in every area of our lives.

empowerment basics

Our lives are so diverse and complex and so many of our decisions are made "on the run" that we can quickly feel overwhelmed by the thought of taking time to dowse for basic decision making. So start slowly, and with one area of your life at a time. The following pages offer focused discussion and practical guidance on a number of strategies for enhancing health that you can explore using dowsing. As you read through them, take the time to dowse for yourself and explore how these different topics might have relevance in your life. You will surely find the time wisely invested.

Far from being an additional, burdensome step in decision making, you will find that the new information discovered through dowsing leads to simple but profound changes in patterns of thought and behaviour, and that even a small investment of dowsing time can send far-reaching ripples into your life. If you like the changes that occur as a result of your dowsing, you will soon find your pendulum a close friend and constant companion. The more that you practise your dowsing, the easier you will find it to frame useful and relevant questions, and the quicker you will find your answers.

One of the biggest and most fundamental shifts in awareness that occurs for many people when they start to experience their lives enhanced by dowsing, is the deep-seated knowledge and understanding that we really *do* know, deep down and for ourselves, what healthy looks and feels like and that we really *can* take the initiative and power to claim that for ourselves. Freedom, self-empowerment, and personal responsibility are the natural consequences of this experience of self-generated, self-guided health and original health is ours to reclaim.

◁ **Honouring and expressing our inner wisdom adds shine and sparkle to everything that we do.**

▷ Sights, smells and sounds that are pleasing or beautiful to us help to affirm our relationship with our environment.

healthy reactions

Moving towards a state of health that is natural, for most of us involves letting go of long established, unhealthy thoughts and behaviour patterns, of limiting and fear-based emotions, and of physical toxins of various kinds that our body has accumulated and stored, unable to rid itself of them. As we do this, we may well experience a cleansing process as the old, blocked energy and physical toxins are mobilized and released for excretion.

This can make us feel physically unwell and emotionally upset. This is a natural part of a constructive healing process and of the return to health, and when it occurs in an

intense fashion it is often termed a healing crisis. This is not something to be feared, but is to be welcomed and embraced. We can see it as a threshold over which we need to pass in order to find a new, more healthy place in ourselves and our lives.

Many of the healing strategies and some of the techniques described in this book may precipitate such a cleansing, detoxifying, healing crisis either in yourself, or in others who you are helping to heal. It may last for a few seconds or minutes, or it may last for hours or sometimes for days. An initial cleansing period of three days is very commonly experienced. Try to ride through it with a gently positive and hopeful attitude, as you will surely feel better for it and feel revitalized when it is over.

◁ Health is supported by those activities which nurture our whole self, that is not only our body, but also our mind and our spirit.

supporting the healing force

To move through this period, it is helpful for us to be optimally supported in body, mind and spirit. The body can be supported by an intake of plenty of water, and a simple cleansing diet of bland, mostly raw whole foods, fresh fruit and root vegetables. Cook by steaming or boiling rather than frying. For the mind and spirit, allow yourself as much rest as possible and gentle outdoor exercise and avoid becoming overly tired.

Spend time engaged in activities that you enjoy. Allow yourself periods of quiet contemplation and meditation, and picture yourself becoming entirely whole and completely healthy.

As you or those that you are supporting move through this cleansing period, energetic balance will gradually be restored and a great sense of vitality and peace will be experienced. We then have an increased ability to deal effortlessly with life's challenges, and health is its own rich reward.

▽ For a healthy alternative, have a glass of juice in place of wine, you can still use elegant glassware.

The food that we eat

"We are what we eat" is a well-worn phrase, but a true one nevertheless. Our physical body is a truly awe-inspiring miracle. Constantly building, repairing, adapting and regulating itself, balancing a myriad chemical reactions and complex biological processes, it has a level of organization and infrastructure comparable to a large city.

Our food provides the wide variety of raw materials as well as the fuel for all of this activity, and comprehensively serving our body's diverse nutritional needs is a key to keeping it functioning at its peak level of health and vitality.

Our body is remarkably tolerant of inadequate nutrition, but only for short periods, our long-term health is inextricably linked to our long-term diet. The experience of being optimally nourished – both by feeding our body all the things that it truly needs and by avoiding foods or other substances that are harmful or toxic to it – is radically different from the experience of simply getting by on a make-do diet based on convenience and circumstance.

Dramatic improvements in mood, concentration, sleep quality, strength, endurance, disease resistance and overall vitality occur when all of our nutritional needs are met. Tailoring our diet to perfectly meet all of our body's needs is a wonderful gift that we can give to ourselves.

finding our optimum diet

There are many resources available to inform us and help us make healthy eating choices. Important considerations include the range, type and quality of food, as well as the balance of proteins, carbohydrates and fats. In addition, we need to ensure we have sufficient fibre, an adequate and balanced intake of vitamins and minerals, and plenty of fresh water. Whatever kind of food we eat, the best quality foodstuff is organic, grown in a mineral rich, living soil, which has not been treated by pesticides or chemicals, and consumed as near fresh as possible. Food preparation is important too, with choices between eating raw or cooked food, and if the latter, how it is cooked.

△ **Dowsing helps us to tailor a healthy diet to cater for our individual needs.**

Learning about food and nutrition is of immense and lasting value. Each one of us is different, however, and it is difficult, even for the well-informed, to fully assess the nutritional needs of a unique individual. Harder still is the challenge of assessing and adapting our diet to keep pace with the constant changes our body encounters at various points in life, such as growing up, pregnancy and breast feeding, changing work and leisure activity, and ageing for example, and the gradual variation in physical activity and food availability that follows the annual cycle of seasonal change.

This is an area of our lives where our inner wisdom can tell us what our intellect can never wholly know, and where our dowsing can act as a tremendously helpful tool and ally, guiding and supporting us in making the healthiest and most life-affirming decisions.

◁ **Generally speaking, food that is raw, fresh and organic has more to offer a healthy diet than over-cooked and processed foods.**

▷ From dietary choice to assessing the ripeness of fruit, a pendulum is a useful tool in the kitchen.

dowsing our diet

Our intuitive self knows exactly what our body needs in its diet for vibrant health. Take some time to sit quietly and reflect on your diet. What did you eat today? Yesterday?

Make a list of everything that you have eaten in the last three days and you may have some surprises – what we actually eat and what we think we eat can be two quite different things.

Take out your pendulum, centre yourself and clear your mind. Be sure to let yourself come to a place of non-attachment - our relationship with food can be very tied up with meeting emotional, rather than nutritional needs. Check your "Yes" response.

"Is it timely and appropriate for me to dowse about my diet?" If "Yes" proceed with questions that are answered by "Yes" or "No".

"Does my present diet meet all of my protein needs? Do I need to add new sources of protein to my diet? Would my protein needs be best met by adding eggs to my diet? Would one egg per week be sufficient to meet my needs at this time? Should I also add other sources of protein?"

You can also use your pendulum to dowse directly over specific foods, checking to see if they are right for your body, either in general or at a particular moment.

diet analysis

Make an overall dowsing analysis of your diet. Here are some pointers to start with:
• Identify any foods that are missing from your diet, any that are present in excess and any that your body would rather not have.
• Increase your daily intake of water to 2 litres/3½ pints per day to improve hydration and to regulate appetite, it also assists toxin elimination which may occur as you begin to reform your diet.
• Start to compile a list of all the foods which your dowsing indicates you need. You can use the table to help you, adding to it until you have a complete checklist.
• The process of tailoring your diet is necessarily a slow one - dowse once a week in this way over a period of three months and keep adding to or amending your list. Keep a diary of the changes that you experience.

dowsing a meal

You can also begin to dowse as you prepare each meal. Although laborious at first, you will find that the process speeds up dramatically as you become familiar with your body's needs and preferences, and you will also develop an increasingly intuitive feel for what your body might like.

"Does this meal contain everything that my body needs right now? Do I need to add more fat and oil? Would a serving of sunflower seeds meet my needs? Is there anything in this meal that my body would prefer to eat less of? More of? Anything that I should eliminate from this meal?"

blessing food

Finally, before you eat your meal, get into the habit of blessing your food. By directing loving energy into your food you can increase its energy level. You will also find that you are more relaxed and enjoy your meal more, putting your body into a happier state in which it can digest and make the best use of your meal.

Hold your hands over your food and visualize golden or silver loving energy chanelling through you and entering the food on your plate. Try dowsing a glass of water before and after a meal, energizing it in this way and see if the taste improves.

DIETARY REQUIREMENTS

A well-balanced diet contains foodstuffs from the three main food groups in roughly the proportions shown, as well as adequate fibre, water, and supplementary vitamins and minerals. Use the table as a starting point for finding your optimum diet, compiled through your dowsing.

protein (c.15% of diet)
high quality sources include: eggs, pulses, soya, quinoa, cheese, meat and fish.

fats and oils (c.15% of diet)
high quality sources include: fresh fish, nut and seed oils.

carbohydrate (c.70% of diet)
high quality sources include: whole grains (rice, oats, whole wheat), green and root vegetables, and fresh fruit.

fibre
high quality sources include: whole grains, nuts and seeds, vegetables and fresh fruit.

water
drink c. 2 litres/3½ pints of filtered, uncarbonated water per day.

minerals
high quality sources include: whole grains, pulses, seeds, green and root vegetables.

vitamins
high quality sources include: nuts and seeds, fresh and raw green and root vegetables and fresh fruit.

subtle energy
all raw, fresh fruit and vegetables, especially green and root vegetables

Food vitality, vitamins and minerals

As well as its physical nutritional properties, food carries the "life-force" or vital essence of the plant or animal that it comes from. This is most intensely present when the food is at its freshest, and gradually diminishes over time and through processing and cooking. Food that has high life-force seems to taste better and gives us more nourishment. Often we find we need to eat less of a food to feel satisfied if its vitality is strong. Food with high vitality adds a shine to our eyes and a bounce to our step.

vitality chart

Dowse over your food to assess its vitality. Because vitality slowly diminishes, a scale is useful. The suggested scale is 1 to 10, with 0 indicating no life-force, and 10 meaning fully vital. You can use the chart shown here, or else choose your own scale and create your own chart. "Is the vitality of this rice higher than 5? Higher than 8? Does it have a vitality of 10?". You will almost surely find that fruit and vegetables just picked will have the highest "score", and wholefoods will also be high on the vitality scale. However, if you compare these with packaged foods that have long shelf lives and additives, their score will be low. Wherever possible eat foods that have a high vitality. To a certain degree, food vitality can be raised by blessing it.

◁ Food vitality varies widely depending on growing and harvesting conditions, storage, packaging and processing. Although subtle and unseen, the vitality of food is a significant part of its nutritional value.

vitamins and minerals

As we have seen, proteins, fats and oils, and carbohydrates, are the three main food groups, and we need an appropriate and balanced quantity of these on a daily basis to maintain and fuel our body. Equally important, however, is our intake of vitamins and minerals.

We need these in relatively small amounts, but their presence in our diet is essential. Minerals are an integral part of much of our body's structure, and both vitamins and minerals are required for many of the chemical and biological reactions and interactions that our body continually performs. Many com-

mon health complaints stem from mineral or vitamin deficiencies in our diet, and supplementing our intake can have dramatic effects.

Ideally, we would obtain our necessary vitamin and mineral requirements by eating an appropriately diverse and balanced diet. Unfortunately, this can be difficult to achieve. Much of the food available to us today is grown in very depleted soils and is then treated and refined in ways which remove the minerals and vitamins from it.

For this reason, we generally need to supplement our diet with preparations of vitamins and minerals. Generally speaking, adults will have their needs met by taking a good multi-vitamin and multi-mineral preparation, plus some extra vitamin C.

Vitamin and mineral requirements are hard to assess other than by the presence or absence of deficiency or toxicity symptoms. Hair analysis is helpful for assessing long-term mineral status. Strands of hair can be sent off for special laboratory tests which indicate how much or how little of particular minerals there are in the body. Toxicity occurs if a vitamin or mineral is excessively present in our diet, as liquid or solid. Mineral toxicity sometimes occurs from drinking water. You can have your drinking water checked for this.

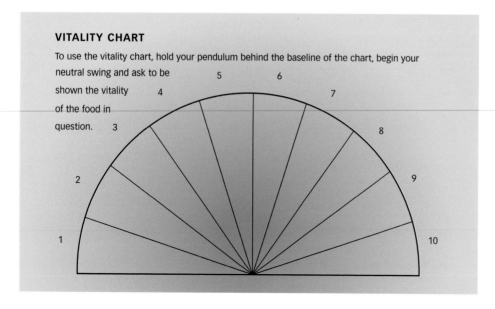

VITALITY CHART

To use the vitality chart, hold your pendulum behind the baseline of the chart, begin your neutral swing and ask to be shown the vitality of the food in question.

dowsing for supplements

A superb way of accessing our inner wisdom regarding our vitamin and mineral needs, and of letting our body tell us what it needs for optimum health is through dowsing.

Centre and balance yourself and check your "Yes" response. "I want to assess my current vitamin and mineral needs. Is this timely and appropriate?". If "Yes" then you can proceed.

"Does my present diet meet all of my vitamin requirements? Would a multi-vitamin preparation be the best way for me to meet my vitamin requirements? Is there one brand which would best meet my current needs? Do I need other specific vitamin supplements in addition to a multi-vitamin preparation? Is there anything else I should take?"

You will find a broad range of vitamin and mineral supplements at health-food stores as well as in most pharmacies. Try and meet your needs from as few products as you can. You may want to take your pendulum with you to the store and dowse discreetly along the shelf to find the best combination of supplements, or you might take a note of what is available and dowse over the list while you are at home.

Dowse for the most appropriate combination of vitamins and minerals for yourself - your dowsing may also indicate that one brand is more suitable for your needs than another brand. Frame all of your questions so that they can be answered fully with a "Yes" or "No", and before finishing your dowsing session, ask "Is there anything else that I need to know about this now?"

Once you have completed dowsing and have chosen your supplements, read the labels carefully and calculate the total doses of each vitamin and mineral that you will be taking. Many nutritional experts feel that the Recommended Daily Amounts (RDAs) currently on food labelling are too low. However some vitamins and minerals can be harmful if taken in excess, so please do not exceed the amounts suggested by the manufacturers, doctor, or other expert on nutrition.

Fully meeting our vitamin and mineral needs has a huge impact on our health. The effect may be noticed within a few weeks, but it is particularly of benefit to our mid to long-term health and may not be noticed for some time. Supplements can represent a sound investment in improving our chance of extending quality of life.

△ **Owing to the diminished quality of much soil, even healthy-looking food may not contain all the vitamins and minerals that our bodies require. Supplements are a way of ensuring that our needs are met**.

Compile a list of the following minerals and dowse over it to find out what you need: calcium, chromium, copper, iron, magnesium, manganese, selenium, zinc, cobalt, iodine, molbdenum, phosphorous, potassium, silicon, sodium and sulphur.

All sorts of factors can affect your need for vitamins and minerals, so dowse to reassess your needs every three months or so to stay up-to-date with your body's changing needs.

▷ **When choosing supplements, dowsing helps us to select the products that are most suitable for our unique needs. Re-assessing these from time to time will accommodate any changes in life or lifestyle.**

The trouble with allergies

Our immune system develops from infancy and is responsible for maintaining the integrity of our physical body. It distinguishes between things that are beneficial or harmful to us. Some things are neither one nor the other, and can simply be ignored.

When the immune system encounters something potentially harmful, it activates various mechanisms for neutralizing or eliminating the threat. Most of the time it does this quietly without our noticing.

the allergic response

An exception to this quiet and efficient functioning is when our body mounts an allergic response. This occurs when the body over-reacts to something benign or minimally harmful as though it were toxic. We may react to things in our diet, the air that we breathe or anything that we touch at home or at work, and experience rashes, poor digestion, sinus irritation and more.

In essence, allergies are disorders in our relationsip with things around us, and are reflected in our thoughts and feelings – body, mind and spirit together.

There are different degrees of allergic response, those which are very minor are known as sensitivities. These mostly go unnoticed, but both allergies and sensitivities deplete our vitality, keeping us from an experience of optimal health.

detecting allergies

There are a number of ways of detecting and working with allergies. The technique laid out here relies on dowsing to detect allergies and sensitivities and desensitizing yourself using the power of the body-mind-spirit connection. It is entirely safe to use and can bring tremendous relief to allergy sufferers and a significant increase in vitality.

Note: this technique is generally successful but cannot be guaranteed. For this reason, even after desensitization, those people with serious allergies should never expose themselves to allergens except under close medical supervision.

◁ **Paints and other chemically-based products can trigger allergic reactions.**

Things that we are allergic or sensitive to are called allergens. To identify allergens in your diet or environment, you can either dowse things as they occur to you, as you meet them, or, more efficiently, you can dowse using lists of possible allergens.

Start by writing out a list of all the main items in your diet, and of all the things which you are in common contact with, at home and at work. This may take some time, but the rewards can be worth the trouble.

Use the list of common allergens shown to help you and add any that you already suspect may cause you trouble.

The more specific you can be, the better. If you find that you have a pollen allergy for example, it is best if you can identify which plant it is from, although you can also work with pollen generally if you do not know.

Centre and balance yourself, check your "Yes" response, and dowse if it is appropriate and timely to dowse for allergens.

If "Yes", dowse down this list or one you have personalized, resting a finger on each item and asking: "Am I allergic or sensitive to this?"

Make a separate list of all the items where your dowsing indicates that you have a sensitivity or an allergy.

▷ **Dietary sensitivities are highly individual, although some, like those to dairy produce are surprisingly common.**

◁ **Reactions to commonplace items may be so long-standing that we accept the resulting diminished health as normal.**

▷ Using the body-mind-spirit connection, we can desensitize ourselves to allergens by holding the thought of the allergen and the desensitizing number, which can be represented on a chart, or just pictured in our mind.

desensitization strategies

It is often the case that although we may be in contact with many allergens, a small handful of key, triggering allergens have a central destabilizing effect on our immune system, and that if we concentrate on these and remedy them, the others will either disappear or diminish to a level that the body can effortlessly accommodate.

Dowse down your list of allergens asking: "Is this a significant triggering allergen for me?" and make a new list of these. Typically at this stage you will have a list of between one and five key allergens.

There are two strategies for working with allergens. One is by avoiding contact with the allergen and can be as easy as making a change in our diet or using a different detergent. Often the allergen is an unavoidable part of our environment, however, and avoidance is not always a practical solution.

The other method involves reprogramming our immune system so that it learns to relate to the allergen in a normal and appropriate way. It is a bit like learning a new response to our fears or phobias.

For each of the triggering allergens, we need to find a desensitizing number. This number represents a dilution at which our immune system can meet the allergen without experiencing an overload. The greater the triggering potential of an allergen, the

more we need to dilute it to comfortably encounter it. This desensitizing number may be any number, but is often between 100 and 200.

Dowse a number for each allergen. Use "More than ...?" and "Less than ...?" dowsing questions to get the number for each allergen. Ask: "Is the desensitizing number for house dust more than 100?" "No." "More than 50?" "Yes." "Less than 75?" "Yes" and so on until you have the exact number.

Once you have all your numbers, sit peacefully and hold the thought of the allergen and its desensitizing number in your mind. Think of each one for a few minutes, 2 or 3 times each day for a week. You can dowse to find out exactly how often and for how long you should do this.

After a week, dowse the numbers again. The desensitizing number typically gets lower - quickly at first and then more slowly over further weeks, until it stabilizes or the allergen no longer has the capacity to trigger your immune system.

Dowse every so often to check which of the allergens on your triggering list you need to continue to work with and to update their numbers.

Continue the practice for at least two weeks to give it a full chance to work. You may find that you can eventually take all the allergens off your list, or that you need to keep up a maintenance with one or two of them. Be guided throughout by your dowsing. Expect to be surprised by the power of your mind to restore health to your body.

COMMON ALLERGENS

Use this list of common allergens to build up a picture of which things you are sensitive or allergic to. Give yourself a score for each positive reaction.

introduced environmental allergens

fertilizer	glues
fungicides	paints
herbicides	solvents
industrial chemicals	varnishes
insecticides	electromagnetic
exhaust fumes	radiation

environmental allergens

animal hair	human hair
feathers	mould
house dust	pollen
house dust mite	insect bites

food allergens

alcohol	sugar
caffeine	wheat
corn	chocolate
dairy produce	tomatoes
soya	tea

Healthy aromas

An active sense of smell seems to have developed early in human evolution, and to have been a primary way in which our ancestors encountered and assessed the world around them. Nowadays, most of us tend to rely in the first instance on our sight and hearing to analyse and interpret our surroundings, using smell as a secondary and for the most part subliminal sense.

We tend only to focus closely on smells that, literally, "catch our attention", either because they are unexpected or strong, or because for some reason they are particularly remarkable to us. One area in which most of us do still use smell in a primary way is in our relationship with food, which is a basic and essential survival skill for all animals.

smells and our wellbeing

Most of the time, smell acts as background information, adding a layer of texture to our world, and influencing not so much our thoughts but our feelings and general sense of wellbeing. Although subliminal, this effect can be profound, rather like background music, which can influence our mood and level of activity even if it is playing quietly and goes virtually unnoticed.

Consequently, many smells are cues for behavioural responses or are associated with particular places and activities. Take for example the smell of a forest or the ocean, of a petrol station or home-baking, of our working environment – these places each

have their own particular smell, and give a cue to our body to wake up, go to sleep, be alert or perform in a particular way.

Some smells have a universal quality in the way that they influence people. Scents are used in spiritual practices to engage the mind in peaceful contemplation and to invoke particular qualities of spirit. Others are used in perfumes for their alluring or aphrodisiac qualities.

The scents of plants are present in oils that the plant creates, and can be extracted in a highly concentrated form. These are called aromatic, or essential oils. Because of their profound effects upon us, plant aromas can be used as agents of balance and healing.

aromatic oils for health

Aromatic oils are known to have been used for healing for thousands of years, and are currently enjoying great popularity.

Most commonly, essential oils are used in a diffuser or burner, added to a bath, or used in massage. Their effects are due to both their scent, and to the physiologically active compounds in the oil which are either inhaled or absorbed through the skin. Essential oils are concentrated substances with medicinal properties. They should be used sparingly – a few drops at a time. In general, aromatic oils are too strong to be used undiluted on the

skin, although some oils, such as lavender, are gentle enough – but even then they should be used very sparingly. Other oils, because of their potency, could be harmful in certain conditions, including pregnancy. Aromatic oils should never be swallowed or taken internally.

USING AROMATHERAPY OILS

In a diffuser or burner: 3 to 4 drops in water to scent a room.

Added to a bath: 4 to 6 drops – but mix them in 5ml/1 tsp of cream or full-cream milk first to help them disperse in the water.

For massage: the oils should be diluted in a massage oil (known as a "carrier" or base oil). Light oils such as sweet almond or sunflower seed are ideal for use as a base oil. Use 3 drops of essential oil to 5ml/1 tsp of massage oil.

By inhalation: 1 to 2 drops in a bowl of hot water.

For localized pain: use hot or cold compresses, soaked in water containing 3 to 4 drops of oil. Squeeze the cloth out then apply.

◁ **Subtle aromas are a powerful background "music" for influencing our mental and emotional state.**

◁ **Flowers help to cleanse and vitalise the air as well as adding their own fragrance and personality.**

Dowsing for aromatic oils

Dowsing is a wonderful aid to guide you in selecting the most appropriate aromatic oils, whether for general wellbeing, to restore balance, or to actively aid in a healing process. Start by asking the following questions: "Would an aromatic oil be helpful in balancing and restoring my health at this time? Would a combination of aromatic oils be best?" If you find oils are suitable, then dowse with your pendulum over your selection of oils. If you have a large selection, you can save time by dividing the oils into two piles and ask: "Do I need any of the oils in this pile?" Once you have selected your oil/s ask: "Is one drop of this oil sufficient? Two drops? Three drops?" and so on until you find out the right dosage for you.

If you prefer, you can dowse from a list of oils, or you might take your pendulum with you when you go shopping and dowse along the shelf to find the most appropriate oil/s for you. If the staff or other shoppers seem surprised or curious, you can offer to teach them to dowse.

△ **1** Centre yourself, clear your mind and enter your state of alert, engaged non-attachment. Check your current signal for "yes". Having established that aromatic oils would be of benefit, dowse over the bottles, identifying clearly which one you are dowsing for each time. A single oil may be indicated, or a mixture of different ones. Try to keep mixtures to five oils or less. You can check your selection by gently inhaling the oils that you have chosen. We are typically pleased and attracted by the scents that our body needs.

△ **2** For massage, add three drops of essential oil to at least one 5ml teaspoon of a carrier oil such as sweet almond oil, sunflower seed oil or other light nut, seed or vegetable oil. For baths, add four to six drops diluted in full cream milk.

△ **3** For personal inhalation, add two drops to a bowl of hot water. To scent a room, add four drops in water to an aromatic oils burner. For a compress to treat localised pain add three drops in a bowl of water, soak a cloth then squeeze out and apply.

GETTING STARTED WITH ESSENTIAL OILS

There are literally hundreds of essential oils. You can start by using some of the ones suggested here but please check with your supplier or an aromatherapy reference book for any contra-indications of oils you are unsure about. Use your pendulum and dowse to see which ones you need and suit you best.

Chamomile
Anthemis nobilis
Soothing and calming, antidepressant. Pain-killing, anti-inflammatory and antispasmodic. Good for muscle aches, inflamed joints, allergies and indigestion. Useful for teething and earache.

Bergamot
Citrus bergamia
Uplifting, good for anxiety and shock. Antiseptic. Useful for oily, or infected skin. Acts as an appetite stimulant. Do not use before going into direct sunlight, can cause uneven tanning.

Lavender
Lavandula officinalis
Calming, soothing and balancing. Antidepressant, aids insomnia. Pain relieving. Helps wound healing. Good for burns, insect bites and stings, muscular aches and pains, and headaches.

Rose otto
Rosa otto
Confidence enhancing. Antidepressant, especially for sexual and relationship difficulties. Helps post-natal depression. Aphrodisiac. Helps regulate menstrual cycle, powerful uterine.

tonic. Tones circulation and digestion. Helps dry skin. Do not use in the first 4 months of pregnancy.

Rosemary
Rosmarinus officinalis
Stimulant. Tonic for nervous system, heart, liver and gall bladder. Relieves muscular aches and pains. Aids respiratory problems, colds, catarrh, sinusitis. Avoid in cases of epilepsy. Not to be used in the first 5 months of pregnancy or conditions of high-blood pressure. Too much can cause the skin to itch.

Tea Tree
Melaleuca alternifolia
Immunostimulant. Antibacterial, antiviral and antifungal. Useful for acne, cold sores, and blisters of shingles and chicken pox. Good for catarrh and sinusitis. Used for warts, verrucas and athlete's foot (apply undiluted, but sparingly).

Caution
Don't use any essential oils for more than 2–3 weeks at a time: alternating oils is always a good policy. Consult a medical practitioner if you are in any doubt.

Flower essences

There is a philosophy that our natural environment has and always will provide us with everything that we need to restore and maintain our health in body, mind and spirit.

In 1930 Dr Edward Bach, an eminent English physician, left his flourishing homeopathic practice in London's Harley Street to pursue his ideal of bringing a simple system of healing within the reach of everyone. Believing that the divine light from which all humans could derive healing was particularly present in the energies of plants, he turned to the flowers of his native land to find remedies for the psychological and spiritual imbalances which he believed to be the cause of all illness. He was encouraged to do this by his experience: he had suffered physical illness and imbalances of both spirit and mind, and had healed himself by finding the relevant flower remedy. He went on to discover 38 remedies in all (often referred to as essences), which are still available today.

vibrational patterns

Although not a dowser, Dr Bach worked in a highly intuitive way with plants. His approach differed from herbalism, where physiologically active constituents of plants are extracted for use in a concentrated form, and also from homeopathy, in which small amounts of an active substance is diluted many times over. Dr Bach's focus was on the very essence of the plant – it's vibrational character or spirit – which he found to be most intensely present in its flowers.

He found the plant's character can be absorbed as a vibrational pattern by water and he began by collecting sun-drenched dew from freshly opened flowers. Later he found it was more practical to suspend freshly cut flowers in water for a few hours on a sunny day, and was just as effective. In this way, it seems that the vibrational qualities of the plant are transferred to the water and held as a memory pattern. These vibrations

△ All plants have a spirit or vital essence which is most strongly expressed in the flowers. The human emotional body is quickly affected by flower essences, and can receive healing and balance from them.

then become available when small amounts of the water – even just a few drops at a time – are ingested. The drops can be taken directly onto the tongue or mixed with a drink.

Flower essences seem to work by influencing our subtle bodies – primarily the emotional body – with consequent healing and balancing effects upon the physical body through the spirit-mind-body connection. Because their influence is not through direct action on the physical body, and because they contain no physiologically active ingredients, the flower essences are completely safe and non-toxic to use, even if taken inappropriately.

Note: The base of the flower essence is often alcohol. If you have a sensitivity to alcohol choose one that has a water or a vinegar base.

◁ Because we are composed of the natural elements of our environment, everything that we need for health is present around us, from plants in the wild to those in our garden.

Dowsing for nature's healers

Flower essences are among the most useful, safe and friendly ways to restore health and wellbeing. They work first on our emotions with subsequent effect on the total body-mind-spirit entity. Powerful yet very gentle, they are completely safe to use at home for treating yourself, friends and/or family. Using dowsing to guide their selection and correct dosage allows us to get the best possible results from using them.

△ **Healing essences can be made from any flower.**

▷ **1** Begin by dowsing whether flower essences would be helpful for dealing with a current concern. Centre yourself and clear your mind, entering into a state of engaged non-attachment. Set your pendulum into its search position and check to confirm your "Yes" signal.

Holding your issue or concern clearly in your mind, ask: "Is it appropriate and timely for me to dowse for this?" If the answer is "Yes", ask: "Would flower essences be helpful and appropriate to use?" If the answer is "Yes", then continue.

Dowse to find out which particular essence/s you need. If you already have a selection of flower essences, you can dowse from these. It is useful to have a full range of flower essences to choose from, but if you don't have the full set, you can dowse from a list or take your pendulum shopping with you, and discreetly dowse for the ones that you need in the shop.

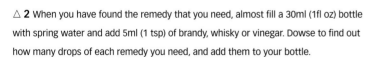

△ **2** When you have found the remedy that you need, almost fill a 30ml (1fl oz) bottle with spring water and add 5ml (1 tsp) of brandy, whisky or vinegar. Dowse to find out how many drops of each remedy you need, and add them to your bottle.

△ **3** Alternatively, for more acute conditions, you can add the drops of flower remedy directly into a glass of spring water. Dowse as before to find out how many drops you need.

◁ **4** When you are ready to take the remedy, dowse to find out how many drops to put in your glass of water. Then take small sips of your drink as required. Flower remedies can work very quickly, see if you notice any change in your mood after taking them.

Creating flower remedies

Since Dr Bach's creation of his first flower remedies, many others have been inspired to follow this path of healing and have developed their own range of flower remedies or essences. Increasingly popular with holistic therapists as well as for home use, there is now a wide and comprehensive variety of flower remedy ranges from around the world available in the shops, each one having its own particular personality. Your dowsing can help you to choose which range is most suited to your needs.

Wherever we live however, nature will provide us with all that we need for health and balance and it is quite likely that the plants you need for your own healing may already be growing somewhere near you, perhaps in your garden or on wild land nearby. To create your own remedies from local sources is a wonderful way to both take an active interest in your health and to deepen your relationship with your environment. At the same time, the process of finding the flowers will simultaneously open a channel for meditation and psychic discovery.

All living things on earth have not only a material, physical form, but one which is spiritual and invisible, and which has its own consciousness. In the world of spirit devas are the nature spirits responsible for the overall growth and health of plants. To

discover which plants we need for our health and wellbeing, we first need to open up a channel to connect with the devic energies of the place where we are living.

Either in your garden, or wherever you feel most drawn to connect with the devas, create a time for quiet meditation, bringing your pendulum with you. You may choose a field, a wood, an open plain, or even your own garden. Wherever it is, find a comfortable spot, ideally where you can sit relaxed with your spine erect.

Centre yourself, clear your mind, and visualize yourself in a column of golden light, supported and protected by your own spirit guides.

When you feel peaceful and balanced, ask clearly in your mind to connect with the deva responsible for plant growth in that area. You may experience visual images or a sense of warmth and peace, it is different for each person, but you will know when you have made a connection.

Now begin dowsing. Set your pendulum into its neutral swing and check your "Yes" signal. State clearly in your mind: "I wish to ask about making flower remedies from local plants. Is it timely and appropriate to dowse about this?" If the answer is "No", give thanks for the connection and try again at another time.

△ **Sometimes we can read the essence of a plant by observing which insects, birds or animals are attracted to it.**

choosing the right flowers

If the answer is "Yes", then dowse to ask which flowers you can use and what their healing properties are. You may wish to search specifically for a plant or plants that will help with an existing concern that you have.

Be careful to frame your questions so that "Yes" and "No" are complete answers, and be open to ideas and suggestions that may occur to you as you proceed. Your intuition will give you information in every way that it can.

Start with a few different plants (not more than three), that your dowsing guides you to work with.

Sit with each of these plants quietly and connect with the spirit of each one, noticing what images and feelings come to you.

Check any ideas that you get with your dowsing, and find out as much as you can about how the plant will be helpful.

If at any time you feel uncertain or insecure, check your "Yes" response, and then dowse: "Is it appropriate and timely for me to continue with this process?" Sometimes we need to proceed gently and with small steps, we can always come back later to gather more information.

◁ **Allow your intuition and imagination to help you tune in to the spirit of the flowers themselves.**

Making a flower remedy

Once you have identified the right plant/s for you, the next step is to harvest freshly opened blossoms on a sunny day. Asking for help and guidance from the devas and also from the spirit of the individual plant, dowse to ask how many blossoms you need to take. This will depend on how much remedy you intend to make and the size and potency of the blossoms.

▷ **1** For ½ litre/1 pint of flower remedy, one to seven blossoms would be typical. Cut the blossoms so that they fall into a glass bowl, ideally without handling them in the process.

Add water to the bowl, about two-thirds of the total volume of essence that you wish to make and enough so that the blossoms are floating. Place the bowl in sunlight.

◁ **2** Next, direct your own loving attention to the bowl, holding your hands over the water as though blessing it, while clearly asking in your mind that the energy of the blossoms be transferred into the water.

Dowse for how long to add your own energy to the water and also how long to leave the bowl in sunlight.

Once your dowsing indicates that the process is complete, give thanks to the spirit of the plant and the devas for their help and remove the blossoms from the water using a pair of clean tweezers. Taking care not to touch the water with your hands as this may disturb and alter the flower essence.

▷ **3** Pour the water into a clean glass jar and add vinegar or spirit-strength alcohol (brandy or whisky are ideal) to stabilize and sterilize the remedy. Add about half as much vinegar or alcohol as water, place the lid on the jar and keep in a cool, dark place. This is your stock solution from which you can make up dosing bottles as needed. It is stable at room temperature and can be kept without losing its properties almost indefinitely.

▽ **Flower essences make a lovely gift for a friend.**

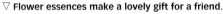

Enjoying life and finding your path

A fully healthy life is one where all aspects of oneself are appropriately energized, and where everything that we do is congruent with our core values and our sense of self. The integration of our mind and spirit into all that we do is essential for good health.

Many cultures have prayers and songs for everything. A sense of the value of the work that we do, with a sense of being present in a wholehearted fashion is an essential ingredient to cultivating emotional integrity and a sense of wellbeing.

There is a story of a traveller encountering three men working on a building site, each one engaged with the same job. He asks them what they are doing. The first replies, "Can't you see? I'm breaking rocks!" The second answers, "Me? I'm earning a living to support my family." The third pauses in his work and tells the traveller, "I'm helping to build this cathedral to the glory of God."

◁ **Integrate the things which bring joy and pleasure into your life, rather than waiting for burn-out to tell you that something is wrong.**

a wellness programme

Many of us drift along in our lives and only focus on issues of health when we feel something is wrong. Wellbeing and vibrant health, in the present day cultural climate, are qualities that need to be consciously cultivated and not left to chance.

It is tempting to allow ourselves to become depleted through the week and then do something healthy at the weekend to make up the balance. Or perhaps we allow ourselves to get depleted through the year and hope to rectify the balance with a week or two of holiday.

An alternative to this boom/bust cycle is to start to integrate health-giving activities into every day even if we believe we don't have enough time or our days are already full.

Begin by identifying everything you would need in your life to feel totally healthy and fully expressed. Take the time to draw up a list and put down everything that brings

you joy and makes your heart sing. Include the things that are of central importance and value for yourself, your family and your community. Don't worry if the list gets long. Make categories under three headings, body, mind and spirit.

Now go through your list and see which items you give lots of energy to, and which ones are being starved of time and attention. You might also consider where most of your time and attention actually does go, is it to areas that are not on your list at all?

Next, see if you can identify the core characteristics of the things that you love to do or feel good about doing. Whether the activities are at home, at work, in leisure or with the family, perhaps a common thread is being with people, or doing things as part of a team. Or perhaps being outdoors is the core component to several activities on your list. By looking through your list in this light, you can generate a smaller, stripped down list of core qualities that are always present in the things that make your heart sing. List these as before under body, mind, spirit headings.

◁ **Be mindful in everything you do, and try to see what it adds, even in a small way, to the bigger picture.**

from threads to strong fabric

The second part of creating the wellness programme is to weave these core qualities into every part of your life. Simply by having a clear idea of what these central qualities are, will take you a long way towards prioritizing your time and energy and doing things where these qualities are most present.

Seek to include more of your core qualities in your existing daily routine. As choices come up for you, consider how many of your core qualities are in each option. Look for ways to maximize your time by weaving activities together. You might find, for example, that activities that you and your partner do separately could be equally met by an activity that you could share, which would weave personal time and core qualities together.

If there are qualities that are not getting much time or attention, look to see why this is. It is possible that you have fears or difficulties around prioritizing them, that they seem out of reach or too self-indulgent.

Look for ways that these neglected areas can be energized effortlessly and without disrupting the fabric of your life. Perhaps they can be expressed in something that you already do, or met in an easier way, or made part of your work or shared leisure time with a partner or friends.

◁ **Creating and using a wellness chart helps to bring our attention in a holistic way to issues of balance in our life.**

creating a wellness chart

Make a chart like the one shown here, covering each area of your life, or use this basic one to begin with.

Set your pendulum swinging backwards and forwards so that it swings into the inner neutral area. Now ask the question: "Which area of my life do I most need to focus my attention on to enhance my health and wellbeing?" The pendulum will continue to swing, but will change the direction of its swing to point to one of the wedges of the half-pie chart.

You might do this two or three times, asking: "Which is the next most important area of my life to focus my attention on to enhance my health and wellbeing?"

With this information, dowse further into each of the topic areas identified, starting with the first and most important. Think creatively about how you can energize this area of your life, and check out any ideas that you have by asking "Yes/No" questions of your dowsing. Let your spirit guide you in making healthy choices and finding healthy solutions from the options available to you.

Once you engage with this practice, you will find yourself making increasingly healthy choices and your life itself becomes your wellness programme.

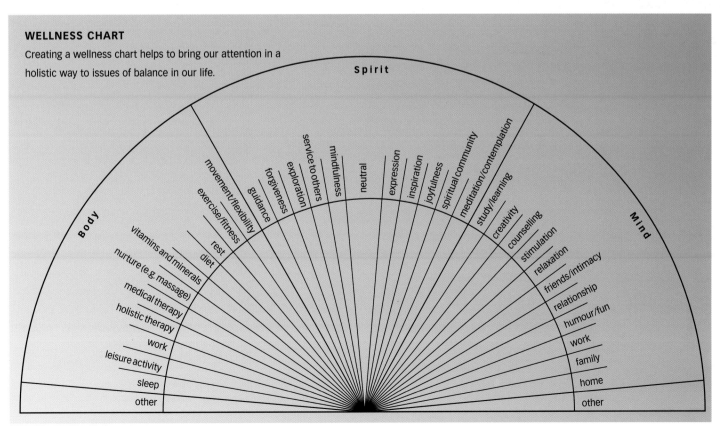

WELLNESS CHART

Creating a wellness chart helps to bring our attention in a holistic way to issues of balance in our life.

Spirit · Body · Mind

movement/flexibility · exercise/fitness · guidance · forgiveness · exploration · service to others · mindfulness · neutral · expression · inspiration · joyfulness · spiritual community · meditation/contemplation · study/learning · creativity · counselling · stimulation · relaxation · friends/intimacy · relationship · humour/fun

vitamins and minerals · rest · diet · nurture (e.g. massage) · medical therapy · holistic therapy · work · leisure activity · sleep · other

work · family · home · other

Vital Healing

"Your intelligence is always with you,
overseeing your body, even though
you may not be aware of its work.
If you start doing something against
your health, your intelligence
will eventually scold you."

Rumi (1207–1273)

The healing gift

One of the great human gifts and mysteries is our ability to channel healing energy, if the need is present and if we open ourselves to do so. What could be more natural than to comfort a child who has fallen during play and hold the place that hurts, even to kiss it better? It is hard to say exactly what exchange has taken place, but the outcome is that the child feels reassured and comforted, and the acute distress and often the pain itself disappears. The body may take some time afterwards to heal itself, but it seems as though, at a subtle energetic level, a healing exchange has already occurred, and the child's psychic and emotional energy becomes directed elsewhere as it returns to play.

Healing is an entirely natural expression of the human spirit, bringing grace and balance to both the channel and the recipient of that energy. It is often associated with a deeply peaceful feeling of engaged compassion. Healing can be practised quite spontaneously and intuitively, or it can be focused through structured and systematized techniques. No one method of healing is necessarily better than another, what is important is to heal in a way that feels natural and comfortable for you as an individual.

There are no rules to follow when healing, but there are a few helpful guidelines to bear in mind, particularly for people who find a vocation in healing and become intensely or frequently engaged with it. Adhering to these guidelines will help healing to occur.

△ **The human desire to comfort and heal is one of the most natural and basic of our instincts, and powerfully affirms our fundamental nature.**

the healing sequence

Your intuition will tell you all that you need to know for healing effectively. Dowsing helps all of us to do our best work.

In the presence of someone who has asked you for healing, centre yourself, clear your mind, and allow your body to be relaxed and alert. Set your pendulum swinging in the neutral position, and then check your "Yes" response.

Ask first: "Is it appropriate and timely for me to be channelling healing energy for (name)?" If the answer is "Yes", put down your pendulum for a moment, and visualize yourself in a column of golden light. Invite healing energy to enter you from the source of healing and love.

You may notice a tingling or vitalizing sensation in your body, or perhaps you can feel an energy pool or bubble between your

GUIDELINES FOR HEALING

• Research and experience shows that true healing works best when we project energy in a completely unconditional form and are unattached to the outcome. Simply channelling unconditional, loving energy to another person supports their spirit in healing and finding wholeness and balance in whatever way is right for them.

• When giving healing, see yourself as a channel through which healing energy can pass, rather than seeing it as coming directly from you. When you are healing, ask that you too may benefit through the process.

• Remain unattached to the outcome of your healing activity, and don't judge the results. This seems strange as one might expect a successful outcome to always be a complete physical recovery from an illness or injury. However, we cannot know or judge the path of another's spirit through the world. Even death is a natural and healthy part of life.

• Be unattached to the nature of the illness or injury of your subject. Whatever we focus our attention upon, we give strength to, and invite into our own lives. When transferring energy hold your focus on the unconditional love that you are channelling.

Channelling healing energy

To be effective in channelling healing energy it is important to pay attention to your own state of well-being. You will need to practice centring and opening yourself to the divine healing energy. One of the most effective ways to do this is through meditation. In addition to this you will ideally need to balance all areas of your life, from the physical aspect to the mental and spiritual aspects.

hands (during the healing, you will project this energy through your hands to where it is most needed). Some people feel the energy strongly in their hands as heat or perhaps other sensations, and others feel little or nothing, but the healing works just as well either way.

Returning to your pendulum, dowse for the optimum positioning of your hands for directing the healing energy. Ask questions such as: "Are my hands needed where the pain is? Around the heart area? Further to the left? Is this the best position now?" and so on, until you find where your hands need to go. Also, dowse to find out whether your hands should be directly in contact with your subject or else a little away from them.

Once you have found the position, relax and visualize unconditional, loving energy flowing into you, through you and out of your hands into and all around your subject.

Dowse intermittently to check if more energy is needed in that position, or if it has absorbed all that it can at present. You may spontaneously feel when the person has had enough at one spot and that it is time to move your hands to a new location (or back to a previous one) or to end the session. Use your dowsing to confirm: "Is there anywhere else that I should be channelling healing to? Is the process complete now?"

Once you are finished, visualize that the energetic connection between you and your subject is ending and then that it has stopped. Then visualize yourself entirely filled with golden light, clean, clear, whole and healthy, and give thanks to the source of healing and love.

Finally, dowse whether a further healing session would be helpful, and if so, after what interval of time, asking: "Would another healing session be of benefit? Tomorrow? In more than three days?" and so on until you find out.

A healing session every third day or so until health is restored is often indicated, but every situation and individual is unique. Allow the intuitive wisdom of your dowsing to be your guide.

◁ **1** Allow yourself to become calm and peaceful, centred and balanced, paying attention to your breathing. Invite healing energy into you from the source of healing and love, visualising yourself in a column of golden light. Ask that you may also receive healing through the process.

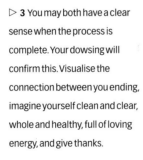

△ **2** Let your hands be guided by your intuition and your dowsing. Move them as your feelings and your dowsing indicate and allow healing energy to flow freely as it will.

▷ **3** You may both have a clear sense when the process is complete. Your dowsing will confirm this. Visualise the connection between you ending, imagine yourself clean and clear, whole and healthy, full of loving energy, and give thanks.

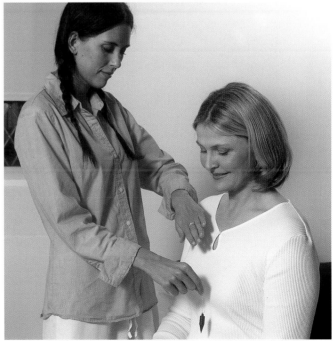

Channel of subtle energy

The spinal column is the central axis of our bony skeleton, and the spinal cord which it surrounds and protects is the central pathway of our nervous system. Additionally, important networks of nerves which co-ordinate and govern many of the body's autonomic activities are centrally placed in front of the spine, and the largest of our arteries and veins carrying blood to and from the heart, lie adjacent to the spine.

A conduit for information exchange, nerve fibres enter and exit our spine, bringing information to and from widespread and corresponding parts of the whole body, co-ordinating the many interdependent systems that work synergistically together. Therapists working with spinal injury understand the far-reaching consequences that damage to the spine will have.

the subtle body

As well as having a physical body composed of matter, we also have a subtle or energy body which consists of vibrational frequency. The subtle body is believed to be an energy field in and around the physical body that holds the pattern and form (inspired by the vital essence or spirit) upon which the material framework of the physical body is organized. This subtle, vibrational body co-exists with and interpenetrates the physical body, and is constantly exchanging information and energy with it.

When any physical injury or illness occurs, an associated and equivalent vibrational imbalance or trauma in the subtle body is also present. It is believed that the healing energies which we

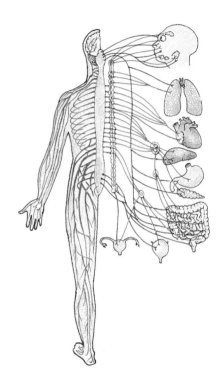

△ The blood supply (left) and the nerves (right) radiate from the spinal column, which is the central axis of our physical and spiritual wellbeing.

channel are of the same vibrational frequency as the subtle body and that they are absorbed and integrated first by it rather than by the physical body.

During any healing process, health and balance is understood to return to the subtle body first, either through its own healing processes or in an accelerated and enhanced fashion through the channelling of healing energy from another source. Once the vibrational pattern is restored, the physical body then returns to health at its own, slightly slower pace.

Identical to its physical counterpart, the subtle body also has the spine as its central axis, the focal point of balance and the centre of organization and information exchange. When studying the subtle body, it is often perceived as having several layers extending outwards from the physical body, or of consisting of several separate but inter-woven subtle bodies which are arranged on the physical body concentrically.

▽ Just as the seeds of this plant radiate outwards, and then outwards again, so the nerves leave the spine and connect with all parts of the body, down to the single cell.

Different traditions give these subtle bodies (or the subtle body's layers) different names and describe them in slightly different terms. One version is that there are seven in number, including the physical, all centred upon the spine. Each one is somewhat larger and of a higher vibration than the previous one, and each is associated with a different level of consciousness. The smallest and most dense is the level of the physical body and the largest and most refined is the level at which we become one with the source of love and healing, or the Divine.

As well as the seven vibrational layers or levels radiating outwards from the spine, it is also considered that there are seven nodal points where energy is focused (generally referred to as the chakras), arranged along the length of the spine, which similarly have resonance with different levels of our consciousness. This reinforces our understanding that the spine is not only the central core of our energetic anatomy but is also a channel of access which allows us to reach every little part of the whole.

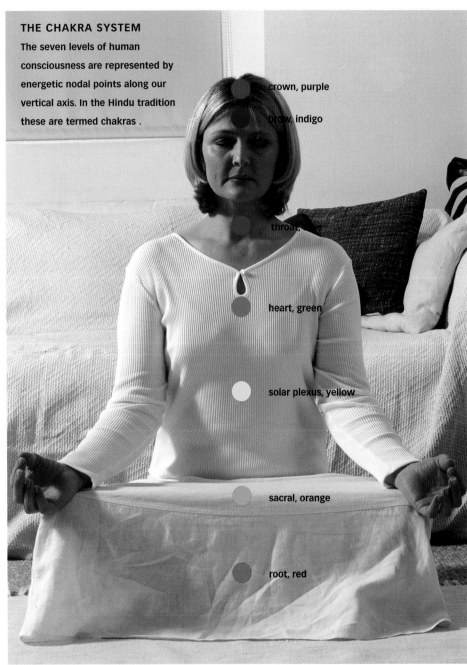

THE CHAKRA SYSTEM
The seven levels of human consciousness are represented by energetic nodal points along our vertical axis. In the Hindu tradition these are termed chakras .

crown, purple

brow, indigo

throat, blue

heart, green

solar plexus, yellow

sacral, orange

root, red

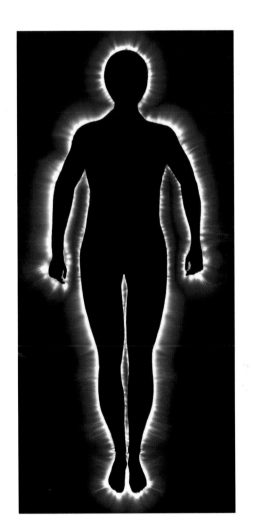

However one may see this, the key for us when engaging in healing is that by holding the spine as our central focus, we can simultaneously channel healing energy to every level and part of the body.

Here at the centre of the body, all levels are equally present, and balance and health restored in one level will facilitate the return of balance and health in each of the others, body, mind and spirit. Truly a divine path for healing.

◁ **One way of imaging the subtle body is through the use of Kirlian photography. This technique creates a picture of the parts of the vibrational energy field nearest to the physical plane – those energies concerned with holding the physical and emotional pattern and form.**

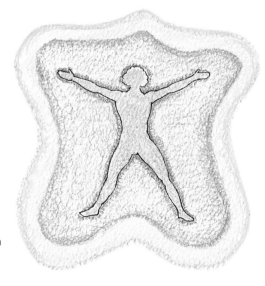

△ **The human aura consists of many layers radiating outwards from the physical body. The size of the aura can depend on mood and place.**

Healing through the spine

We know now how to call on healing energies and how to channel them through our hands. We are also familiar with the spine as a key focus for directing our healing attention.

To most effectively focus our healing through the spine we need to know at exactly which level the energy can be most easily absorbed and have the greatest benefit. Dowsing offers itself as a valuable ally in each part of the process, guiding us until the optimum energetic transfer has occurred.

In the presence of someone who has asked you to channel healing energy for them, begin by centring yourself and clear your mind. Allow your body to be relaxed and alert. Set your pendulum swinging in the neutral position, and then check your "Yes" response.

Ask if it is appropriate and timely for you to be channelling healing energy for this person. If you receive a "Yes" response, visualize yourself in a column of golden light, and invite healing energy to enter you from the source of healing and love.

Next, ask of your dowsing whether your healing should first be directed towards the spine. If you receive a "No", follow your intuition and ask further questions of your

△ **All patterns repeat throughout nature. Like a person, each leaf has a central axis or spine, giving structure and allowing the exchange of nutrients and information.**

dowsing to find out where to put your hands. Once you feel and have confirmed with your dowsing that sufficient energy has been transferred there, ask again if you should now focus on the spine. If "No", continue to find the next hand position. You may find yourself completing the session without ever having focused on the spine.

When your intuition and dowsing say to bring your attention to the spine, begin by asking whether your hands will be together over the same place. If "Yes" then you have only one spinal level to find. If "No" then you have two spinal levels to find.

You now need to find the correct positions for your hands. To do this, move your dowsing hand slowly down the spine, asking to be shown where to place it. Use your middle finger as a pointer when you get close to the exact level as before. Apply your other hand in the same way, and visualize the transfer of loving, healing energy while relaxing and allowing yourself

◁ **Like the tree and waterfall, energy and information in the spine moves from sources below us and from sources above us.**

to remain engaged, compassionate and unattached. This process of finding the correct spinal level can go quite quickly once you are familiar with it and after a while and with experience, many people find that they can easily sense or feel the right level intuitively, only relying on their dowsing for confirmation or checking their accuracy.

moving on

After a while you will feel that the energy is slowing down or no longer seems to be flowing through your hands. This could be the moment to move on or to end the session.

Use dowsing to confirm that sufficient energy has been transferred to the spinal level where you are working, and then dowse to find out if there is more to do elsewhere, (and if so where to direct the energy), or if the session is over.

When your dowsing indicates that you are finished, visualize the energetic connection between you and your subject ending and stopping.

Visualize that you are entirely filled with golden light, clean, clear, whole and healthy, and give thanks to the source of healing, light and love.

Conclude by dowsing to see if a further session is needed, and if so when the best time would be.

▽ **Just as the sun has a cycle, so healing has a cycle; the ebb and flow of healing allows mind and body to integrate fully with spirit.**

Scanning the spine

1 Start your pendulum swinging in its neutral position and hold your free hand out with an open palm, close to your subject but a few inches from their physical body.
▷ **2** Start with your hand at the level of the very top of their head, and, without ever physically touching them, scan progressively downwards, following the line of their spine all the way down the centre of their back from their head, down their neck, mid-back and lower back until you reach the level of their tail bone at the bottom.

▷ **6** Next ask your dowsing if your hand should be placed on the person's physical body. If "Yes", place your hand against their spine, covering the indicated spot with the centre of your palm.
If "No", start with your open hand next to the spine and slowly bring it outwards until your pendulum indicates the appropriate distance at which to work.

Begin with your subject sitting comfortably, try and put them at their ease so that they are relaxed and open to the healing.

◁ **3** As you do this, hold clearly in your mind the question: "Is this where I should place my left/right hand ?" (depending on which is the free scanning hand).
4 As you go, you will find at some point that your pendulum starts to swing into its "Yes" response. Depending on how quickly your free hand is scanning down the spine and whether you are looking at your scanning hand or your pendulum when the "Yes" response occurs, you will have a close idea of the spinal level that you are being invited to channel healing to.
5 To get the exact level, go over the approximate area again, starting just a little above where your "Yes" response began, but moving more slowly down the spine this time and pointing with a finger. If you hold your pendulum close to your scanning finger, you will find it easier to see when the "Yes" response develops, marking the spot for you.

Spinal dowsing

We have discovered that the physical and subtle bodies share their central core in the spine, and that they constantly exchange energy and information. We have also seen that imbalances in the pattern of the subtle, vibrational body can manifest in the matter of the physical body.

One place where imbalances are commonly exchanged and shared is between the levels of the mental, emotional and physical bodies. When an unresolved issue is triggered (such as a particular fear for example) by an event, memory or such like, the mind may interpret incoming information as overwhelming, and instead of processing and releasing the emotional energy created, it simply transfers it to the physical body which contains and protects it by contracting around it and walling it off. Thus held, re-activation of the painful emotion is avoided by minimizing the amount of energy flow and movement in that area of the body. Physically, this becomes a localized point of muscle contraction and spasm. Repeated similar experiences can build up further local contraction, gradually affecting our posture. Over time, the muscles become habituated to this contraction and mistakenly adopt this compromised posture as normal.

One can also read the mood or overall demeanour of a person by observing their

posture, recognizing the characteristic and distinct emotional holding patterns which gradually and progressively influence and overshadow their basic character and personality. Gentle healing for body, mind and spirit releases the mental and emotional tension and allows the person to return to their original, natural posture.

The compromised posture can impair many different systems, including the critical nerves that enter and exit the spine at the affected level. Working directly at the physical level where the imbalance is stored, the posture of the spine can be gently helped to correct itself and the postural muscles on

◁ When sending healing energy to the spine, you will need to dowse to find out which areas on the back need your loving attention.

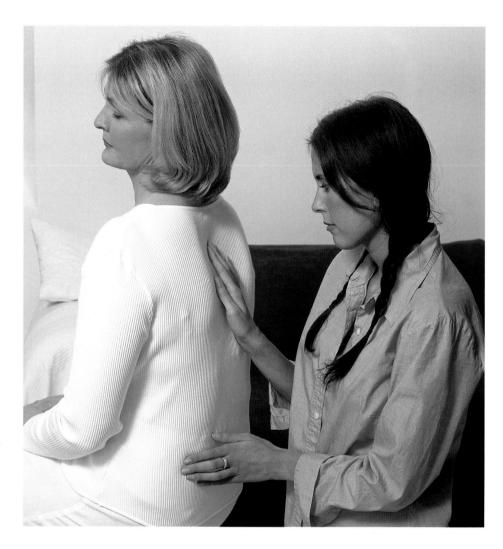

△ Bringing gentle, loving energy to areas which have been traumatized, whether physically, emotionally or at other levels, helps the process of integration and healing to occur.

either side of the spine encouraged to release the knots. This aids a return to normal function, including that of the related nerves and associated information channels.

In the process of restoring the physical body to greater flexibility and natural balance, intensely emotional memories may surface of the original hurt which has been stored in the body, and through emotional release the person is brought to a sense of deep peace and healing. Holding a safe space while this emotional unburdening occurs is an important and key part of the healing process.

restoring flexibility

Helping the spine to regain its natural state of balance by reconnecting with the tight shut-down places, so as to restore energy flow and flexibility, is the goal of many therapies. Some of these are highly technical and require extensive training. Others are delightfully simple and easy to learn.

One technique for helping the spine remember its most healthy posture relies on dowsing to identify points on the spine that need to be brought to the body's attention, and on the subject's own gentle movement to restore an appropriate level of flexibility.

First check the "Yes" response of your pendulum and then, in the presence of someone who has asked you for healing, dowse whether it is timely and appropriate to channel healing for them.

If the answer is "Yes", then ask if they have any known disease or injury of their spine. If they are not sure, you can check with the pendulum. If they do however, it is best to channel healing energy to the appropriate area of the subtle body and not directly to the physical one. Having checked it's safe to work directly on the spine, ask your dowsing whether helping their spine to adjust its posture is

timely and appropriate. If "Yes", scan slowly down the spine from the crown to the tail-bone as before, this time asking clearly in your mind: "Please show me the fulcrum point for the necessary postural adjustment."

When you have found the right place, put down your pendulum and place your thumbs gently against the spine as shown, one on either side.

Now, while keeping your thumbs in place, invite your subject to slowly and gently, in their own time and without going beyond their comfortable range of motion, go through four simple movements.

Dowsing the spine

Start with your subject sitting comfortably relaxed with their spine straight and tall, breathing slowly and deeply. Then invite them to perform the following movements.

The size and range of movements is not important. These should all be done gently and slowly and feel entirely comfortable to your subject. Do not let them strain, hurt or over-extend themselves. The gentle touch of your thumbs will call their spine to an awareness of that level and give it the necessary information to direct appropriate healing there. A combination of gentle postural adjustment, massage and healing guided by dowsing is a tremendously versatile and effective way to restore health and balance to the central axis of our physical and subtle bodies.

◁ **1** Ask your subject to arch her back around where she feels the touch of your fingers, and then return to upright.

▷ **2** Then ask her to bend forwards and in so doing pushing your fingers backwards, and then return to upright.

◁ **3** Your subject then rotates around to the right, turning her head to look over the right shoulder, then returns to upright. This rotation is repeated to the left, looking round over the left shoulder.

▷ **4** After the spinal movements, dowse to see if there is another postural adjustment required, and if so follow the same procedure as before. You may find only one to be necessary or perhaps several. Now dowse to see if gentle massage is required to help soften the holding pattern of the muscles. If indicated, massage in small circles into the large muscles immediately to each side of the spine. You will feel these gradually soften and let go under your fingers. Dowse to see where and for how long this should be done. Finally, dowse to see if channelling healing energy to the subtle body is also required. If "Yes", proceed with this as before until the session is complete.

Healing through hands and feet

We have discovered that healing energy can be directed to a number of different levels, and that the interconnection between the subtle and physical bodies can allow indirect as well as direct attention to be brought effectively to areas of imbalance and impaired health.

The physical body can be very protective of its wounds and imbalances, particularly those that hold grief or intensely upsetting emotional energy, and will only allow itself to release these if it feels respected and safe. Often, one of the main tasks of healing is to search for the place and level where healing is invited and welcomed, and to identify how the body's many interconnected systems, physical and energetic, can most easily absorb and relate to healing input with the least resistance or reaction. Dowsing is an invaluable tool to guide us as we look for this open door.

For this reason, it is helpful to have a number of different strategies for channelling healing, and to allow dowsing to indicate which is most appropriate in any given situation.

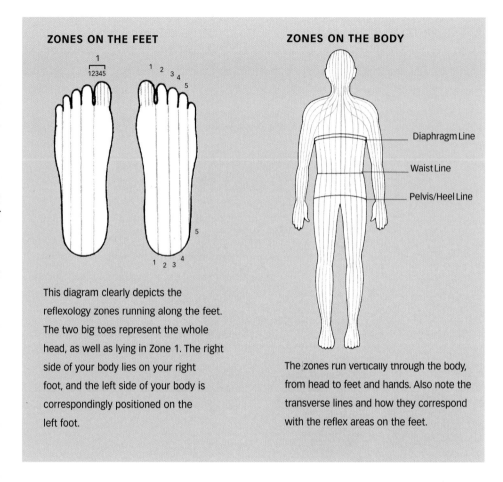

ZONES ON THE FEET

1
12345

1 2 3 4 5

5

1 2 3 4

This diagram clearly depicts the reflexology zones running along the feet. The two big toes represent the whole head, as well as lying in Zone 1. The right side of your body lies on your right foot, and the left side of your body is correspondingly positioned on the left foot.

ZONES ON THE BODY

Diaphragm Line

Waist Line

Pelvis/Heel Line

The zones run vertically through the body, from head to feet and hands. Also note the transverse lines and how they correspond with the reflex areas on the feet.

reflexology

This is a gentle and non-invasive healing technique which is easy to learn and safe to use and can be guided entirely by dowsing.

As with the other techniques that we have learned, it is based on a philosophy of all things being connected and interwoven, and that energetic transfer occurs at non-physical levels.

Reflexology, or reflex-zone therapy as it is also known, is based on the understanding that there are subtle energetic connections between the hands and feet and all other parts of the body, including the internal organs and their related physiological systems. A form of holographic map of the body is laid out on both hands and feet, each side of the body being mapped out on the corresponding hand and foot. By stimulating the appropriate part of the hand or foot, an energetic transfer is effected to the related point in the body.

Trained reflexologists can use their knowledge of these maps and their related areas and points to focus their healing attention and also to help them in diagnosing problem areas, even before these have shown up as apparent physical problems.

Without specialized training, we can make use of these energetic associations by allowing our dowsing to guide us.

◁ **Using reflexology on the hands is suitable for children as well as adults.**

The physical and subtle bodies are inextricably linked. Look and you will see this in all things.

dowsing the hands and feet

It is easier to apply dowsing techniques to the feet because they are bigger than the hands, and their reflex zones are a little further apart. However, some people are very self-conscious about their feet, in which case working with their hands may be preferable.

In the presence of someone who has asked you for healing, centre yourself and clear your mind, and with your body relaxed and alert start your pendulum in its neutral swing and check your "Yes" response.

Ask if it is appropriate and timely for you to be channelling healing energy for this person. If "Yes", ask if it is most appropriate to focus your healing through reflexology.

If "Yes" again, ask your subject whether they would prefer you to work on their hands or on their feet. If you will be working on their feet, they will need to remove their shoes and socks.

Before you start, visualize yourself in a column of golden light and invite healing energy to enter you from the source of healing and love.

Begin with the right hand or foot. Start by simply holding it in a loving way until the level of intimacy feels comfortable and relaxed. Then place the thumb of your non-dowsing hand against the sole of the foot or the palm of the hand and begin dowsing.

With your pendulum in its neutral swing, state clearly in your mind: "I wish to channel healing energy through the reflex zones of this hand/foot. Please guide me to the point where healing is most needed."

Then begin a series of directional questions to guide your thumb to its first point. "Is the first point to the left of where my thumb is? To the right? Nearer to the toes/fingers? Is this the right point?"

At each point, direct a firm but gentle pressure inwards with your thumb while visualizing a transfer of loving energy. Apply the pressure steadily for several seconds and then release and reapply. Make sure you don't dig in with your nail.

Dowse after about 20 seconds to find out if sufficient energy has been transferred. If it has, ask if there is another point for you to work on. Occasionally you may be guided back to a point a second time.

Continue until your dowsing indicates that you are finished with that foot or hand.

◁ **Dowse to find the reflexology points on the hand or foot which require your attention.**

Hold it in a supportive way to complete your interaction with it, then transfer your attention to the left hand or foot.

When the session is complete, visualize the end of the energetic transfer, and filling with golden energy which is clean, clear, whole and healthy. Give thanks to the source of love and healing, and dowse to establish if and when a further session would be appropriate.

You will find that with a little practice you can quickly and easily guide your thumb from point to point. There are reflex points on the upper and lower surfaces and the sides of the hands and feet, as well as on the sides, fingers and toes.

△ **Apply firm but gentle pressure to the points indicated for 10 to 20 seconds, then re-check.**

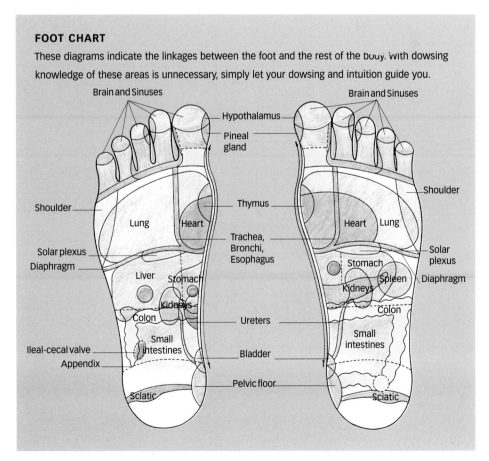

FOOT CHART

These diagrams indicate the linkages between the foot and the rest of the body. With dowsing knowledge of these areas is unnecessary, simply let your dowsing and intuition guide you.

Brain and Sinuses · Hypothalamus · Pineal gland · Brain and Sinuses · Shoulder · Thymus · Shoulder · Lung · Heart · Heart · Lung · Trachea, Bronchi, Esophagus · Solar plexus · Solar plexus · Diaphragm · Stomach · Diaphragm · Liver · Stomach · Spleen · Kidneys · Kidneys · Colon · Colon · Ureters · Ileal-cecal valve · Small intestines · Small intestines · Appendix · Bladder · Pelvic floor · Sciatic · Sciatic

Absent healing

Both healing and dowsing seem to work on principles that are not limited by time and space. We can dowse for something that is not physically present with us, and we can send healing energy to a person who is somewhere else at the time.

We can only speculate about why this is so, it would appear that at the level of spirit, there is a holographic or unified energy field that allows us to perceive and interact with all things simultaneously, regardless of our relative positions in the time-space continuum. Whatever the reason, however, it is familiar and accepted practice for healers and dowsers to not only work with their subjects when they are physically present but also to work with them when they are somewhere else.

This presents a wonderful opportunity. Either by using a natural period of quiet time that occurs during our day, or by setting time aside that we can be sure will be peaceful and uninterrupted, we can focus healing energy on friends and loved ones in need, wherever they may be and whatever they may be doing. Similarly, we can extend our practice to any number of people who

⊲ Set time aside in a place where you can enter a quiet and meditative state without being disturbed. Lighting a candle provides a focus and sets a peaceful tone.

have requested healing from us. Many healers maintain an absent-healing list, communicating with people by telephone or letter, and keeping them on the list until healing has occurred and health has been restored again.

performing absent healing

Begin by creating a peaceful setting for yourself where you will not be disturbed. Some people like to create an altar space to help relax and focus the mind, the presence of a candle, some flowers, and perhaps some

incense or anything else that may assist in focusing your mind towards loving and healing thoughts, can all be helpful. Have your pendulum to hand, your dowsing will help to guide you through the process.

Having settled yourself, focus for a while on your breathing and allow yourself to become thoroughly peaceful and relaxed. Ask for guidance, support and protection from the source of love and healing. State clearly in your mind that you wish to perform absent healing, and visualize yourself sitting in a column of golden light, completely energized, clear and balanced.

Dowsing with your pendulum, ask if you are ready to start absent healing. If the answer is a clear "Yes", then you can proceed. If it is a "No" or qualified by a "But ..." check to see if you are fully centred. It may be that you are not in the right frame of mind to be doing absent healing, or it may be that the timing is not right for some other reason. Take some more time to relax and centre yourself, and then ask again. If your dowsing still tells you not to proceed, then leave the absent healing for another time.

If your dowsing tells you that you are ready to start, than you can begin to tune-in and start healing.

⊲ A photograph can help to tune-in and focus on the person we are sending healing to. A hair sample or other personal item will also work.

tuning-in

Before you can send distant healing, you need to tune-in to the recipient. This is rather like giving a dog a piece of clothing that someone has worn so that it may follow their scent. We need to pick up the scent of our subject. Some healers do this using a photograph or a piece of the person's hair. Others are content with a name and address, perhaps with a birth date and any other personal details that will help to uniquely identify that person. For people that we know well, we can often tune-in simply by thinking of them.

As you tune-in, dowse to see if it is appropriate and timely to be sending them absent healing. If "Yes", begin to send unconditional love to them. A simple visualization of that person surrounded by and in a column of golden light works beautifully.

Do not be distracted by anything that you know about the person or their concerns, and do not hold any attachment or judgement to the process, or the outcome.

Hold the image in your mind for a minute or two or until you feel complete. Dowse to see if more energy is needed. If not, move on to the next person to whom you wish to send absent healing. Between each person, focus for a few moments on your own breathing and re-visualize

△ When sending healing, visualize your subject filled and surrounded by healing, loving energy. Be unconditional and unattached to the outcome of your healing. It is not always possible to know what outcome is best for each person's spiritual path.

▷ Just as electrical impulses can travel over almost infinite distances, so healing energy can be directed to someone who is not present at a healing session.

yourself in your own column of golden light, in which you are energized, balanced and healthy. After healing you should feel refreshed, calm and healthy, if you do not, seek help from someone more experienced.

When you have finished the session, fill yourself with loving energy and let go of the energetic attachments to others. Visualize yourself clear, balanced and whole and give thanks to the source of love and healing.

Absent healing is simple and powerful. As well as helping individuals in need, we can send unconditional love to places and situations that need healing. Sometimes it can help to create miracles.

Earth Energies

"Every continent has its own great spirit of place. Every people is polarized in some particular locality, which is home, the homeland. Different places on the face of the earth have different vital effluence, different vibration, different chemical exhalation, different polarity with different stars: call it what you like, but the spirit of place is a great reality."

D H Lawrence (1885–1930)

The spirit of place

A concept held by older, less materially focused cultures and by some indigenous peoples around the world today is that of the spirit of place. The Romans called this the *genius loci* and often personalized it and conceived of it in anthropomorphic terms, much as they did their pantheon of deities who inhabited both heaven and earth.

For the dowser, this is an easy reality to enter. Having developed an awareness of the connection between body, mind and spirit and gained an understanding that the subtle body holds the intrinsic energy field for the denser physical body, one can extend this perception to appreciate the subtle energy field, or spirit, present in all things.

interconnectedness

The relationship between the subtle and physical body, or the interconnectedness between spirit and matter, applies equally well to trees and plants, to birds and fish, even to rocks and rivers, as it does to human beings. While all of these things have a physical body and therefore a subtle body, the different layers or levels of the subtle body are developed to differing and individual degrees, according to type. For example, the

◁ **The collective consciousness is very strong in many species, particularly herd animals.**

subtle body of a rock is very different to that of a bird or tree, and different again to that of a human being.

The etheric layer of the subtle body, that is, the level closest to the physical body, is the western equivalent of the eastern chi or qui (pronounced chee), and is present in all things. It holds the vibratory energy field and gives both pattern and form to physical matter. The layers of the emotional and mental bodies, respectively holding the consciousness of emotion and thought,

are present to varying degrees, however. The mental body for example, so intensely present and developed in a human being, is minimally present in rocks and minerals, where it has a more diffuse and collective quality. A more developed but still largely collective energy field at the mental level is present for different species of animals that live in groups, some of which show a very strong herding mentality.

places of character and personality

Surely we are all familiar with places that seem special to us. Whether a corner of our garden, a forest clearing or an awe-inspiring mountain top, each of us has been touched by the special and individual qualities of places that we know or have visited.

Often, our experience of visiting these places is similar to that of spending time with a dear and close friend, and our emotions are touched. We can feel inspired or calmed for example by our encounter with a particular spot, and may even describe the character of the place in very human terms: we speak of places as being warm and friendly, or cold

◁ **The power that spirit of place has to move and inspire us to great deeds is familiar to us all. It may be found anywhere, on a hill or by a stream.**

and hostile, peaceful and serene, or disturbed and restless. Although these terms can be applied to the literal, physical characteristics of the place, we are more usually describing our experience of that place, how it made us feel, rather than what it was actually like. It's something we experience more in our stomach and heart rather than in our head. In these cases, we are describing our encounter with the spirit of place.

Humans have intensely developed mental and emotional energy. We have the capacity for self-reflection and the ability to exercise free will. However, our energy body is tiny in comparison to that of our surroundings.

We are all familiar with the way in which our mood is gradually influenced by the tone of music playing in the background. Similarly, our moods and thoughts and many of the circumstances that we take for granted and react to in our daily lives, are defined and patterned by the background, ambient energy field of the place in which we find ourselves. The energy field of place has enormous psychic mass and presence.

At the largest of earthly scales, one can conceive of the energy field of the earth itself. This great spirit is often referred to as Gaia, the spirit of the planet, our home and hostess for the duration of our earthly life here.

Clearly, our relationship with the spirit of place is inevitable and ever-present and is perhaps our most primary and defining relationship. Certainly as we explore issues of personal health, and examine our relationship with every part of who we are and what we do, the relationship we have with place, whether healthy or unhealthy, is one which has immense impact and importance in our life.

◁ **Being still and offering our imagination to the landscape allows us to experience its subtle nature more fully. This creates harmony and balance within and can give a wonderful sense of wellbeing and contentedness. A little time spent in this way is valuable to everyone.**

the spirit of environmentalism

Our awareness of environmental issues, including resource limitation, water, air and soil, sound, light pollution and issues of biodiversity, is now creating many and far-reaching changes in cultural attitudes and behaviour towards the planet.

At a purely basic level of survival, we have become aware that we are fouling our nest. Much of the thinking of the environmental movement, however, comes from the same material consciousness that has created the current problems, and even wilderness areas are seen in terms of recreational or aesthetic resources, possibly containing plant species that can be exploited for human medicines or cosmetics. Also, such places are designated special and different, and although we may take care of these, we have less regard for other, supposedly less significant places.

Sustainability is now seen to be essential, but we are approaching it in material, technological and economic terms, many of which are fundamentally incompatible with

the very nature of sustainability itself. So-called primitive cultures have achieved sustainability for thousands of years in their landscapes, even in those areas that are farmed. If we cannot also achieve this, something is missing or wrong, in our approach.

When we look for the core differences between the attitudes of indigenous peoples and the attitudes of our industrialized nations, one of the central factors is an awareness of and reverence for the spirit of place itself. Each day, we are in constant and intimate contact with the earth, exchanging not only air, water and food but also etheric, emotional and mental energy. We may have forgotten, but it is truly a relationship between spirits.

If we were to hold this awareness of and respect for the spirit of place, the conclusions we would draw and our behaviour would be markedly different from those arising when an awareness of spirit is lacking. This applies equally, whether we are speaking at an individual or at a global level. Perhaps a central key to our short and long-term health therefore, lies fundametally in our relationship with the spirit of place.

▽ **Water is one of the embodiments of the powerful elemental forces that move both through ourselves and all things around us. The other elements are air, fire and earth.**

The spirit of the earth

The anatomy of the earth's subtle body is a subject of great fascination, and an area where science and spirituality, folklore and legend meet. We can learn a great deal by comparing it with similar, but smaller energy bodies, such as that of a person.

flowing chi

In Traditional Chinese Medicine (TCM) much attention is given to the flow and distribution of chi around the body. Chi is a Chinese word for subtle, etheric energy, and their understanding is that this is present in every part of the body, animating and vitalizing the physical structure. Practices such as t'ai chi cultivate and balance this energy, with great benefits to health and wellbeing.

While present throughout the body, chi is recognized to have its own circulatory system of meridian lines. These follow connective pathways and distribute chi to every part of the body.

Health suffers when one or more of these chi-paths becomes blocked and energy stagnates or, contrastingly, becomes over-stimulated, causing an excess of energy. The resulting imbalance becomes manifest in mind and body.

To restore and maintain a healthy balance of chi, TCM works on nodal points along the paths, where energetic input at these points can apply leverage to the path as a whole. Acupuncture is the practice of working upon these nodal points with needles.

dragons in the landscape

Many people believe that this characteristic of chi circulation and distribution is fundamental to every energy system, including that of the earth. According to the Chinese the chi-paths of the earth's subtle body have traditionally been known as dragons.

Dragons inhabit every landscape. Typically described as having the body of a serpent, the scales of a fish, the wings of a bat and the claws of a bird, they symbolize the energy that is present in all animals and throughout nature. They bring the etheric energy through the land, making it available to serpent and fish, bat and bird.

△ **The movement of water, both overground in rivers, and underground in natural aquifers, is central to the energetic anatomy of a landscape.**

▽ **Nodal points on the web of the earth's subtle body have long been recognized as places of energetic focus, and are used to balance the fields of energy from the surrounding landscape.**

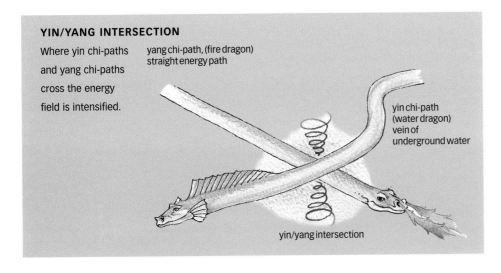

YIN/YANG INTERSECTION

Where yin chi-paths and yang chi-paths cross the energy field is intensified.

yang chi-path, (fire dragon) straight energy path

yin chi-path (water dragon) vein of underground water

yin/yang intersection

Sinuous and mercurial by nature, their energies fluctuate and change with sunrise and sunset, with the waxing and waning of the moon, with the passing of the sun through the seasons and with the deep, quiet cycles of planetary time.

Nomadic cultures followed the seasonal rise and fall of energy in the landscape, knowing both the location of the nodal points on the dragon paths, and the times at which the intensified etheric energy at those places would be most active. As nomadic people began to settle and turn their attention to agriculture, they developed a more fixed relationship with the landscape, remaining in the same location all the year round. They then found it expedient to tame the local dragons, pinning them down and stabilising their energy at the nodal points in order to heighten and balance the surrounding energies, so as to keep them throughout the year.

The legacy of this elegant technology is seen in the standing stones and stone circles of the British Isles and northern Europe, the pyramids of Egypt, the temples of ancient Greece, the sacred sites of Central and South America, in fact, all over the world where agriculture has flourished, the dragons have been tethered and cultivated. By contrast, in landscapes where the nomadic lifestyle has not been given up by the indigenous people, the power centres remain less worked by human hands, and the dragons continue to visit still of their own accord, on more seasonal terms.

▷ **Whereas agrarian cultures tamed and tethered the natural world, nomadic peoples left power centres untouched, and timed their visits to co-incide with the ebb and flow of elemental forces.**

yin and yang chi

Drawing further on the traditional Chinese understanding of these elemental forces, we can begin to discern different kinds of dragons around us, and to become aware of their various qualities.

We can start by observing yin chi-paths and yang chi-paths. Yin and yang are not terms of absolute description, in the way that right and left or up and down are. Rather they are terms of relative comparison, in the way that we would use more and less or higher and lower for example. They can be applied to anything that is dualistic, having opposite, or complementary qualities.

Something with a yin nature is relatively quiet, receptive, of an absorbing, introspective nature. This has the quality of the womb, which takes and nurtures the male seed,

transforming it and creating new life in the quiet darkness. Something with a yang nature on the other hand, has a relatively active, expansive, penetrating and expressive quality much like that of male sexual energy.

Some chi-paths are by their nature yin, and others by their nature are yang. The Chinese make no distinction between human and landscape chi, and refer to the yin chi-path as the white tiger and the yang chi-path as the azure dragon in landforms.

Where the yin and yang chi-paths meet, particularly if this coincides with nodal points on one or both paths, then the etheric energy is most intensely present in a multiplied and interwoven form at that point. These places are known as power-centres, and are sites of intensified spiritual observance and practice.

more and different dragons

This Chinese system is not the only system of energetic classification. The West recognizes its own dragons or energy lines, which are as old as those of the East and all are older than human classification. In addition to energy or ley lines of different magnitudes, which form more or less rectilinear grids across the earth, the form of the land and the geological characteristics below the surface all bear an influence. In addition, there are also energy paths for each of the elements: earth, air, fire and water.

Energy awareness

Knowing that we are surrounded by energy patterns of various kinds, it is a good idea to have an awareness of the way in which they may effect us. Just as our health is related to the quality of food that we eat and the quality of the air that we breath, it is also related to the quality of chi that we are exchanging with the etheric energy field around us.

We know how we become slowed down and relaxed by a glass of wine, or stimulated and speeded up by a cup of coffee. We tend to feel tired and sleepy after a heavy meal, whereas a light salad affects us very little, taking less energy to digest.

Human beings are exquisitely sensitive to the surrounding etheric energy field. Changes in our mood and energy level can be influenced by the predominant energy of our immediate environment. The effect of being in predominantly yin chi slows us down, rather like the glass of wine or heavy meal. Predominantly yang chi on the other hand, acts like coffee, stimulating and speeding us up.

These effects increase with the intensity of the etheric field, and are more extreme the more strongly the etheric field is polarized to yin or yang.

This means that a high-intensity, highly polarized etheric field, such as that carried by a large dragon line of either yin or yang nature, will affect us much more and much more quickly than a low-intensity etheric field. Chi-paths that are small and relatively-weak, are composed of more evenly balanced yin and yang energies.

Although affecting us mainly at a subtle energetic level, our mood, thoughts and physical energies are all coloured by the spirit of place due to the body-mind-spirit connection, with resulting influence on our health. Furthermore, the longer that we spend in any one place, the greater will be its effect upon us.

These effects can be good, bad or indifferent for a human being, depending on how well matched we are to the places where we spend our time. Some places are

△ **Some locations naturally emanate a calming atmosphere of repose and tranquillity. We are often drawn towards them in times of stress.**

more or less beneficial generally, and some particularly significant for individuals. By contrast, the subtle energy field of other places, or of particular points or areas within them, may be damaging and harmful.

◁ ▷ **Some trees and plants are indicator species for earth energies owing to their sensitivities. Fruiting trees thrive in balanced energy fields and do poorly with excessive yin chi, whereas other species, such as fungi prefer yin chi fields.**

⊲ Cats are lovers of yin chi spots, whereas dogs prefer a balance with a slight prevalence of yang chi.

geopathic stress

The modern term used for stress on our health caused by earth energy is geopathic stress. This is not a new idea however. The Roman historian, Plutarch (*c.* 45–125 AD) stated: "Men are affected by streams of varying potency issuing from the Earth. Some of these drive people crazy, or cause disease and death, the effect of others is good, soothing and beneficial."

Other historical figures who have commented on this include Michel Nostradamus (1503–1566). He wrote: "Where plants perish and animals are absent, there you should not live, the place is unhealthy. You will experience disharmony and lose your poise. When you,

however, find the place where happy, vital and healthy people live, and many old folk are in good health, then stay there, you will soon do without medicine or physician. The mysterious forces of the Earth will make you healthy."

Geopathic stress does not only affect human beings. If it did, we might wonder if it were only an imaginary phenomenon. The effects of chi-paths and of the background etheric energy field also extends to plants and animals. Much can be learned about the energetic qualities and anatomy of a place by looking at the growth and health of its plants and the movement and sleeping or nesting patterns of both wild and domestic animals.

Some plants and animals are lovers of yin chi. These include many of the medicinal herbs, mushrooms, members of the nightshade family and ivy. Insects and burrowing animals are generally yin chi lovers, and cats tend to seek out and spend long periods on yin chi spots.

By contrast, other plants and animals do not tolerate strong, unbalanced yin chi and prefer more yang in their immediate environment. These include fruiting trees, beech trees, roses and geraniums, and vegetables

that come to a head above ground. Birds, horses and dogs are also in this category, along with human beings.

Some species can tolerate quite wide extremes of yin and yang chi. Notable in this category are oak, pine and sycamore trees.

If we allow ourselves, we can all pick up on the feel of a place in a broad and general way. Using dowsing, however, we can learn to read and interpret the particular characteristics of chi polarity, intensity and flow in a very focused and specific way, thereby refining and enhancing the quality and health of our relationship with our environment, large and small.

△ Wild growing plants and animals express the spirit of the landscape that they inhabit, and close observation allows us to read the book of nature .

⊲ The health of plant and animal species that have similar energetic preferences to humans, are good indicators for us of the nature of our work and domestic environments.

Dowsing the earth's energies

We can use our pendulum for much of our dowsing in relation to earth energies, but it is also useful to use another of the basic dowsing tools, the L-rod.

the L-rod

This dowsing tool, so-called because of its shape, can be constructed from any material. They can be easily made at home by cutting and bending a coat hanger into the necessary shape. You will need a pair of rods, one for each hand. Mostly used for searching for things while the dowser moves around, they can also be used for "Yes/No" questions in a sitting or standing position.

dowsing with an L-rod

Find a comfortable posture, with the spine erect and shoulders relaxed. Hold the shorter part of the rod firmly but gently, near to vertical, without touching the longer, horizontal part of the rod. Your forearms should

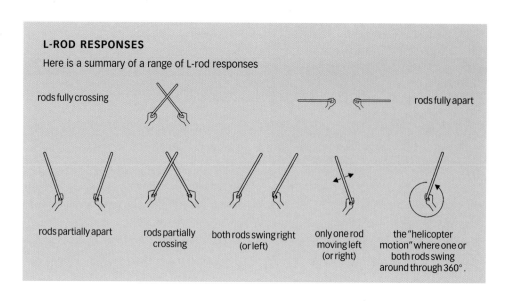

L-ROD RESPONSES

Here is a summary of a range of L-rod responses

rods fully crossing

rods fully apart

rods partially apart

rods partially crossing

both rods swing right (or left)

only one rod moving left (or right)

the "helicopter motion" where one or both rods swing around through 360°.

be approximately horizontal, your elbows bent at around 90°. Your hands should be comfortable, probably about 30cm (1ft) apart.

Practice your "Yes" and "No" movements until they seem easy and familiar. To find your "Yes, but ...", go all the way over for your "Yes" signal, and then come a third of the

way back towards neutral asking for the signal. Repeat this process to find your "No, but ...". Lastly, with your rods in neutral, ask for your "Unanswerable question" response.

As with the pendulum, if you do not get automatic responses, you can programme pre-determined movements for your rods.

establishing "Yes" and "No" responses

The two basic L-rod responses are rods-splitting-apart and rods-closing-together. See what you get when you try to establish your "Yes/No" responses.

1 Hold the rods pointing straight out and away from you, parallel with each other. This is the neutral, or search position.

2 Then, keeping the rods the same distance apart, move them over to the dominant side of your body (if you are sitting, then this can be over your knee). As you do this, state clearly and simply in your mind "Please show me my response for 'Yes'". See what the rods will give you for a signal.

3 Having done that, go back to your middle, neutral position, and then go over to the opposite side stating "Please show me my response for 'No'", and observe what this response will be.

directional dowsing

This method is primarily used for tracking the path of dragons, places where they cross or for finding lost items, whether it is a ring, the way out of a wood or to a particular place. It is a very simple technique and very quick and effective when you are searching for a direction.

1 Stand in the centre of the dragon holding one rod out at arms length, pointing away from you. (If you are looking for a direction to a place, it does not matter where you stand.)

2 Slowly turn your body through 360° while asking "Please show me the direction in which the dragon flows, (or in which the lost object can be found)". As you turn, the rod will seem to stick and continue to point in one direction. This is the direction you need.

3 Turn to face the direction, place your L-rods in the search position and ask "Please show me when I arrive where dragons meet (or where my lost object can be found)." Walk forwards in that direction until you get your "Here it is!" response.

searching for dragons

Now that we are familiar with L–rods, we will use them to discover dragons.

To begin you will need to be centred and grounded. Clear your mind, and visualize yourself in a column of golden light.

Standing comfortably with your rods in their neutral position, state: "I wish to dowse for earth energies", then ask: "Is this timely and appropriate?" If the response is "Yes", then proceed: "Please show me any energy paths of significance to my health." Now walk forwards at a slow but steady pace.

When you reach the first path, your rods will start to split apart as though meeting something solid like a wall. Once they are completely apart, you have arrived at an energy line. This is your "Here it is!" signal. (You may find instead that the rods cross – this is an equally valid "Here it is!" signal.)

Although this response may be the same as that for your "Yes" or "No", in this context it is simply showing you the location of the dragon as requested.

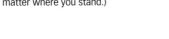
▷ Often where a line or node of earth energy is found, the place will have an intensified character or particularly capture our attention. It is not until we know about earth energies that we understand why this is.

the anatomy of dragons

Each energy path will have two edges and a middle. Sometimes, the larger ones appear to have several edges on each side, somewhat similar to the layers of the human subtle body, lacking only the final, physical layer.

Step back until your rods are in neutral position and then, ask "Please show me the nearest edge of this energy line", and dowse forwards until you find it.

Step back and return to neutral once again and then ask to be shown the furthest edge of the line, dowsing forwards until you find that. Some lines are very narrow, while others are several metres or feet across. Having defined the edges of the line, you can also dowse for the centre of the path.

Next, ask "Is this a yin chi-path?" "Yes" or "No" will tell you its polarity, and then ask "More than ...?" and "Less than ...?" questions to establish its strength on a scale of 1 to 10.

Finally, we wish to know its direction of flow, and the path that it takes through the space. To track the energy, either step sideways dowsing into the edge or centre repeatedly until you have traced out the extent of the path, or use the directional dowsing technique.

Dragons and auras

One of the ways that we can understand and assess the effect that different chi-paths have upon us is to observe the changes in one of the layers of the human subtle body, known as the health aura.

This layer is a sphere around us, typically found between 45cm (18in) to 1m (3ft) out from our physical body. It is observed to expand and contract in a dynamic and flexible manner depending on our current level of personal vitality and the presence or absence of any stressful or beneficial influences upon us.

◁ The dragon is the symbol of energy in motion, whether it represents the body of the earth or the body of a person.

dowsing for auras

To do this you will need two people, one to dowse, and one to be the subject of the exercise.

To begin, both people need to get clear and centred, and visualize themselves in golden light.

Next, place your L-rods in search position and state: "I wish to dowse for changes in the health aura of (name)". Ask: "Is this timely and appropriate?"

If "Yes", first have your subject stand in a neutral spot, that is somewhere where you can't find any dragons.

Stand about 3m (10ft) away from your subject, facing them. With your L-rods in search position, state clearly "Please show me the edge of (name's) health aura".

Walk towards them until your rods swing apart. This is the current position of their health aura. You may be able to feel it with your hands, a very subtle sensation like feeling the edge of a soap bubble.

dowsing on a dragon

Now, stand the subject on the edge of a yin chi-path, at a right-angle to the energy flow. They should be facing away from the centre of the path, with its edge running under the middle of their feet.

Have them stand there for about a minute, noticing any sensations in their body, or changes in mood.

Now, re-dowse their health aura. You are likely to find that it has contracted towards their body.

Following this, stand them on the centre of the path, again at a right angle to the flow, the energy moving either left to right or right to left around them.

Have them stand on the centre of the path for about a minute, noticing any sensations in their body, or changes in mood.

Re-dowse their health aura again. This time, you are likely to find that it has expanded outwards.

Repeat this exercise with a yang chi-path. Again ask your subject to notice their feelings, moods and any sensation they may have in their body. Then observe the effects on the health aura, both at the centre and at the edges of the path.

◁ L-rods are useful tools for dowsing the aura as they will give a very clear response. The aura is affected by earth energies and you can use the rods to dowse for both.

finding intersections

Where dragons meet, their energies merge and enhance each other, creating and intensifying the etheric field and magnifying their effects.

There are very many tiny chi-paths all over the surface of the earth, almost like the lines that go to make up our fingerprints, or the web a spider weaves. This is the earth's capillary network, an etheric web or matrix, distributing chi in an even, gentle manner to every point on the surface of the planet. Most of these lines are so tiny that they do not have a directly significant effect on our health.

Only the larger chi-paths and lines of the energetic web will cause immediate changes in our health aura, and these are the dragons that we are concerned with. If you dowse simply for any chi-paths or lines of dowseable energy you will find very many tiny lines. This is why we should qualify and ask to be shown chi-paths of significance to our health when looking for dragon intersections.

To find a chi-path intersection, use the L-rod directional dowsing technique. As you are following the flow of the chi with pointed L-rods, ask your dowsing to show you a chi-path intersection. Walk forwards until you get a "Here it is!" response.

▷ Tiny chi paths cover the surface of the earth like the strands of a spider's web.

▷ Tiny chi paths cover the surface of the earth like the strands of a spider's web.

assessing crossing dragons

Having found the chi-path intersection, identify the edges and middle of each path, and the polarity, strength and direction of flow. Using your ten-point scale (use "More than ...?" and "Less than ...?" questions with your "Yes" and "No" dowsing) you can also find the individual and combined strength of the two lines. (You may need to go above ten on your scale for combined strength, as the effect of crossing paths is often multiplicative rather than additive).

Place your subject on these intersection points and dowse the effects on their health aura. Yin-yin intersections often reduce the health aura to a very tight, contracted area close in around the physical body, yang-yang intersections moving the health aura further out than usual.

Where the yin and yang paths meet we find the greatest expansion of all, sometimes pushing the health aura out by several metres or yards. This is a consequence of the synergistic, creative energy available when the opposite qualities combine. These synergistic points are known as power-centres.

clearing and grounding

Chi-paths can have dramatic effects on us, and at the end of this exercise we need to clean, clear and ground ourselves.

First find a neutral spot and visualize and affirm that you are clean, clear, full of golden light, perfectly healthy and whole.

When you have finished, dowse to ensure that your subject's health aura is returned to its original size or larger – if it is diminished use one of the healing techniques that we learned earlier to restore and balance their energy.

▽ On nodal points the energy of the health aura may be greatly enhanced and magnified.

Geopathic stress

Geopathic stress is best considered as a dysfunction in the relationship between person and place. It has two basic causes.

The first cause of geopathic stress is when we spend extended periods of time in etheric energy fields which, by their nature, are simply not conducive to human health.

The majority of these are cases are of people exposed to strong yin chi-paths which, being of a relatively more receptive nature than the human etheric body, absorb, drain and deplete our subtle energies. At a mental level this causes fatigue, poor concentration, impaired communication and diminished tolerance for challenge and stress. At an emotional level the effects are feeling low and introverted, and at a physical level, of immune system depletion. Very often, biological cycles are also disturbed.

Ideally, building sites are dowsed before construction begins to ensure a healthy environment for humans. If a building has been constructed on imbalanced or yin chi-paths, it will not be healthy unless the basic nature of the energy present can be repatterned.

The second cause of geopathic stress is when an otherwise benevolent and healthy energy field becomes stressed and traumatized, and the chi-flow is disturbed, blocked or imbalanced. This is typically the result of traumatic changes to the surface of the landscape such as quarrying, excavation, or new construction projects. The effects on us are similar to being exposed to strong yin chi-paths. In this case however, healing needs to be applied to restore health and balance to an otherwise healthy place.

assessing and working with geopathic stress

It is possible to enter a creative dialogue with the spirit of place. If timely and appropriate, and supported by the place, our strongly held and clearly focused thoughts can influence and repattern the etheric field. This allows both for healing and repatterning of the basic nature of the earth's subtle body to occur in a gentle and respectful way.

Let us for example assume that we are assessing a small space – perhaps a room that we have as our main living area – where we will spend extended time on a daily basis. Before dowsing, clear and centre yourself, and visualize yourself in a column of golden light connecting you with the source of love and healing, and check your "Yes" signal: "I want to find out about the energy in this room. Is this timely and appropriate?" If "Yes", then ask: "Are there any energies in this room that are detrimental to human health?"

If so, find out if they are detrimental because of their nature, or because of a trauma of some kind.

healing traumatized energies

If the chi has been traumatized, there is likely one or more blocked, stagnant or overly stimulated chi-paths running through the space. Let your dowsing guide you to where to work.

Place your hands where your L-rods indicate, much as you would when directing healing towards a person.

Visualize yourself channelling healing energy from the source of love and healing, asking that the etheric field receive whatever healing energy that it needs to regain a state of health and balance, peace and vitality.

Dowse intermittently to see if the process is complete. It may require several healing sessions over a period of a few days or even months, the earth's cycles of time are slower than those of a person.

Monitor its progress until you are satisfied that it is remaining healthy.

Be sure to ask that you also receive healing through the process, and at the end of each session, visualize yourself filled with golden light, clean and clear, whole and healthy. Give thanks for the healing that has occurred and end the connection.

◁ **Use L-rods to dowse inside buildings to check for the presence of geopathic stress. If possible, dowse a plot of land before you buy it to assess whether it is compatible with human health or not.**

Repatterning energy

If you find a chi-path in your space that is, by its nature, detrimental to your health, you will need to ask the spirit of place that the energy be redistributed. Remember that the energy itself is neither good nor bad, and that something that may be harmful to us, can be helpful to other species. If we approach energy that is detrimental to humans as something undesirable we might logically think we should try to eradicate it from the planet. However, if we do, we would be removing habitat for half the species of the earth! This consciousness is already widely present in our society, and projecting this at a spiritual level can have very damaging consequences.

▷ **1** Hold your pendulum and begin dialogue with the spirit of place by saying: "I wish to dialogue with the spirit of place here. Is this timely and appropriate?" If the answer is"Yes", continue by stating: "I wish to spend time in this space and need the energy here to be supportive to my health." Ask: "Are you willing to repattern the energy here to be supportive of my health?" If "Yes", ask: "Are you able to repattern the energy here to be supportive of my health?" If it is, it may be able to do this itself or it may require your loving energy to help it to do so.

If the spirit of place is not willing to repattern the energy to support your health, then you may ask it to suggest an alternative place.

◁ **2** If it is both willing and able, make a special request, almost like a prayer:

"I request that the energy in this space be repatterned at this time to be supportive of human health at every level, and that it may remain so for as long as may be the divine will".

This request focuses your intention in a respectful and responsible way that will initiate the changes that you need.

If the spirit of place is willing but is not able to repattern the energy field for you, ask if it can do so with your help.

If it can, repeat the prayer above while directing your loving thoughts into the space, visualizing golden light entirely filling the whole space.

▷ **3** Once your dowsing indicates that the repatterning has occurred, give thanks to the spirit of place, ask a blessing for the place, and end the healing sequence as you have before.

Sometimes the repatterning may take hours or days. Check with your dowsing to see if it needs further help. Once it is complete, dowse the space again to assess the location and nature of the energies present.

It can seem strange to speak with something that we cannot see, but let yourself engage with love with the spirit of place. It has been a long time since our society did this with care and humility, and the consequences have been terrible. If the spirit of place will support you, you will experience immense personal benefit from living in an entirely healthy space.

Space clearing

Geopathic stress affects us primarily at an etheric level, the layer of energy nearest to the physical. Problems can also occur however, in other layers of the earth's subtle body, particularly the emotional and mental levels of energy and consciousness.

This follows our understanding of the body-mind-spirit connection, and of the intricate correlation between the energetic anatomy of all things, whether person, plant or planet.

Most often when a place or area becomes traumatized at the level of emotion or thought, it is as a direct consequence of intense and emotionally traumatic human activity. The most classic example of this is on previous battlegrounds. Often when we visit such sites, we are aware of the intense effect they have upon us, powerfully impacting our mood and our thoughts, often for days, even weeks after our visit. The atmosphere at these places is almost tangible, and it is not hard to imagine ourselves being there at the time of the event.

negative consequences of place memory

It is not healthy for a place to hold such memories. In health, energy is free to move and flow. Emotional and mental trauma creates frozen, disintegrated pockets of energy in space and time.

One consequence of intense place memory is that similar events can occur in a repeating fashion in that location as people resonate with the etheric field, and become influenced by the thoughts and feelings held there. This can occur anywhere that traumatic events have occurred, in the distant past or in recent times. Serious examples of traumatizing place memory include abuse, rape and murder. Places that have witnessed such events are not healthy for further human habitation until the energy at these levels has been cleared and rebalanced.

The emotional and mental levels are not separate from the etheric, and information can pass in both ways. Thus, a very yin or stagnant etheric field, or traumatized chi-

△ **Space clearing cleanses and re-integrates the mental and emotional energy in a place; this is a powerful and important healing process.**

paths from landscape disturbance, can invite human behavioural responses that will in turn place trauma into the emotional and mental field. Truly, all things are connected.

Having learned to work with chi-paths and the etheric layer, we need next to learn how to bring peace and healing into the related layers of emotion and thought.

space clearing

Healing at this level is becoming known as space clearing. When working to bring a place into a state of peace and balance, the chi-paths and other patterns of the etheric layer should generally be addressed first. If they are not addressed, the space clearing is unlikely to be fully effective.

As with our previous healing work, be guided by your dowsing. The clearing, centring, and visualization of golden light before and after these exercises is very important. It is easy to resonate with energetic problems and disturb our own subtle body when dowsing or healing a person. It is even easier for this to occur when working

◁ **Mental and emotional energy can be held as place memory for long periods of time, touching the thoughts and moods of those who visit.**

▷ **Dowsing will help you to assess the need for space clearing and will guide your healing process.**

with disturbances in place, because the energy field of place has so much more psychic mass and presence than that of a person. Be disciplined about cleaning and clearing before and after you work, and ask that you may also be healed through the process.

If you find after a healing process, either with a person or a place, that you are feeling ill at ease or out of sorts, take time for personal healing and cleansing or, better still, ask someone else with healing and dowsing skills to do this for you. It is good for healers and dowsers to support each other in this way.

Whichever method we decide to try, the most important part of space clearing is our intention for it to occur. Use any tools that feel comfortable to you in a simple and authentic way. It can be powerful to use combinations, particularly if all four elements are represented.

We can also clear space without tools. Simply sit and quietly pray for the space to be healed, visualizing golden, loving, healing energy entering, filling and restoring health and peace to all energies present.

△ **There are many tools and techniques which can be used to focus our intent and to help us in space clearing. Use whatever feels most natural to you and appropriate for the space that you are working with.**

USING THE ELEMENTS

Space clearing can be achieved in many ways. All of them share the common intent that any trauma held in the place be gently released and the energy dissolved and reintegrated into the system in a harmless and healthy form. We can enhance and focus our intention for this to happen using any tools or techniques that feel authentic and helpful. Traditionally, these are considered within the elements of earth, water, air and fire.

earth
• Salt is a classic cleanser of energy. You can leave salt in a room in a dish overnight or for a few days and then dispose of it outside to remove detrimental energy and return it to the earth.
• Eggs are also effective space clearers. Leave one overnight in a traumatized room and the egg will absorb any detrimental energy present. Dispose of the egg outdoors for the earth to recycle.

water
• Water from holy wells carries naturally healing energy. You can also bless water yourself by channelling healing energy into it.

• Adding salt to water improves its clearing properties, and adding flower essences is extremely effective for healing the place memory.
• Sprinkle the water around, pour it on the ground, or spray it into the air through an atomizer.

air
• Burning incense (powder or sticks),aromatic oils or cleansing herbs releases their healing energies into the space.
• Sage, cedar, lavender and rue are all good cleansers. You can burn them in a dish and send the smoke into all parts of the space with your hand or with a fan or feather. In the native American tradition, the use of sage in this way is often called smudging.
• Healing and cleansing sounds such as chanting, singing, bell ringing and rattling, also come under the element of air and can be used in space-clearing rituals.

fire
• Whether the fire of an individual candle flame or a large bonfire lit outdoors, fire is a powerful cleanser and transformer of energy.

Landscape Synergy

"...some places differ from one another in their tendency to breed better and worse human beings ...of all these places, those territories which would differ the most would be those that have some divine presence in the winds and are under the care of demons, and hence receive those who come to settle each time either graciously or in the opposite way."

Plato (c. 427 – 347 BC)

Living with the spirit of place

We have been introduced to the concept of the spirit of place, and considered the subtle energy anatomy of the earth and the nature of the etheric, emotional and mental levels of the subtle body. We can now dowse to find and assess chi-paths, work with healing to restore balance within these fields, and endeavour to create a healthy environment for ourselves. It remains now to weave these threads together and place them in the context of everyday life.

the return of power

The reason that we are unfamiliar with many of these concepts and lacking even a common language to discuss them is because of the extraordinary personal power that this awareness brings to us.

Knowing where the centres of etheric energy are in the environment gives one the ability both to influence the consciousness and the spirit of the landscape and to draw on its power for personal use. They are nodal points on the earth's energetic web, open channels for the bilateral exchange of energy and information.

▽ **Everywhere, whatever the location, has its own special spirit of place.**

Any intention that we bring to such places, will be greatly charged and energized. Historically, for purposes of religious and social control, access to and knowledge of these sites was closely guarded by those in power and authority. In recent times, an understanding of their nature has been almost entirely lost or forgotten.

The return to holism leads us back to the spirit of the land however, and now we can learn about, gain access to and interact with the intensified energies of power-centres and enter conscious dialogue with the spirit of these places.

the sacred relationship

In modern times, we have grown increasingly fearful for the safety and wellbeing of our spirit here on earth, and have learned to relate to the spirit of the land with anxiety and distrust. Spiritually protective of ourselves, a consciousness of fear and scarcity has resulted, leading to disrespectful and exploitative behaviour in our relationship with the environment.

Far from its being our hostile enemy, we are in sacred relationship with the spirit of the landscape, which has nurtured us and holds a place for us within it. Generously and

△ **It is important to remember to live with a landscape and appreciate it for its uniqueness.**

selflessly it offers us everything that we need, not only physically but also emotionally, mentally and spiritually. We can regain this sacred relationship simply by changing our attitude to one of love, respect and engagement.

The human spirit has been on a long journey through the darkness of separation and introspection in order to know itself. Now it is time to look outside ourselves and to reconnect in sacred relationship with all the other members of the universal family.

tutelary spirits

One of the gifts offered to us by the spirit of the landscape is to tutor us in relationship both with ourselves and with all that is outside us. For this reason, the spirit of place has often been known as the tutelary spirit. Each place in the landscape holds a particular consciousness for us to engage with and experience, and has lessons, challenges and teaching experiences to offer us.

Most of us are familiar with the way that phases of our life are associated with periods of time spent in a given location. We mostly think of these periods in terms of the activities that we were engaged with during that

▷ Every stirring of the human body, mind and spirit takes place and is held within the greater context of the landscape.

time, whether growing up, going to school, college, having our first job and so on. But the changes that each move brings are much deeper than simply the outward changes. We learn and grow in a place until we have received what it has to offer us – the teachings our spirit needs on its journey – and then we move on, naturally attracted to the next teacher, the next tutelary spirit.

This process of growth and learning can be greatly eased and made more joyful if we engage with it in a conscious and celebratory way rather than ignoring it or resisting all change as being fearful and painful.

the power of imagination

To receive help, tutoring and guidance from the world of spirit, all that we need do is to ask for it. Tutelary and other spirits may not interfere with human free will, but perhaps a good use of our free will is to ask respectfully for help and support in meeting life's many and perplexing challenges.

Having asked for guidance, we need then to pay very close attention to the information that we receive in return. This can come to us in many ways: as synchronous events, as unexpected change, as things that we read, as dreams and ideas, even as work or people we meet. Spirit moves in mysterious ways. The most powerful tool that we have in our psyche for dialogue with the spirit world is our imagination. We have long been led to distrust and discard this precious part of ourselves. To reclaim the power of our direct, personal connection with spirit we need to reclaim the power of our exciting and imaginal reality.

Through dreams, images and inspiration of every tone and colour, our imagination is the creative canvas for us to receive ideas and understanding from the unseen worlds, and upon which we can visualize, create and project our own energies and intentions out into the world.

In some primal cultures, the tribal elders are charged with the responsibility of dreaming the future for both the tribe as a whole and for the generations that will follow. The elders are highly respected members of the community, having accumulated wisdom and experience through their lives. Theirs is the honour and responsibility of the dreaming which is considered to project an essential guiding energy thread into the future. This will safely and harmoniously lead their tribe through periods of adversity and connect them in sacred relationship with the spirits who will safeguard and guide the people on the journey through time.

returning to personal

In this way we are invited to expand our awareness and take a role of responsibility and leadership in our life. Whoever we are, wherever we may be, we are in sacred relationship with the tutelary spirits of time and place that we have, however unconsciously, been attracted and drawn to in order to support us through the journey of life. Open your imagination and your consciousness to engage with them in dialogue. Pay close attention…

▷ Tutelary spirits vary widely in character, and may correspond to the landscape in which they choose to reside. Ask yourself why you are here now? – what is here for you to learn? – what do you have to offer in return?

The spirit of a home

In one study, people were asked to list their most stressful life experiences in order. The results of this showed that the most stressful event of all was to move to a new home. This tells us a great deal about our relationship with the place where we live and which we identify as home.

Our home is the place with which we establish a primary bond of intimacy and identity, and because we spend so much time in our home location and allow ourselves to be so open and vulnerable there, the state and nature of its subtle energetic environment is a core and fundamental factor in determining our overall health.

dowsing your home

The practice of dowsing will help to deepen your awareness of the nature and character of your home, and orient you to high and low energy spots and the flow of chi through it. It also gives you a means of dialogue with the spirit of place.

Begin by greeting the spirit of place. You can use either your pendulum or L-rods for the opening dialogue of "Yes" and "No" questions and answers, and your L-rods for identifying and tracking the energy paths through your home.

Clear and centre yourself, and visualize yourself in a column of golden light. Introduce yourself first. State the nature of your relationship with the place, such as if you own or rent or are visiting, and your intentions in regard to the place, whether it is only a home or also your work place, how you intend to develop and so forth.

"I am (name) and this is my home. I live here with my family and wish this to be a safe and nurturing place to live. I wish to communicate with the spirit of place here. Is this timely and appropriate?"

If the answer is "Yes" then go on. "Is this a safe and healthy place for me to live? Is there anything that I need to know about the energy here? Is any healing required in this space? Are there any chi-paths of health significance that run through this space? Are there any power-centres here?"

Gather as much information as you can, dowsing with "Yes/No" questions. Once you have an overall feel for the energy field, dowse your home room by room with your pendulum or L-rods to find out the peace or otherwise of the energies present, whether any healing is needed, and what the overall polarity and field intensity is using your ten-point-scale.

△ **One way to deepen our relationship with the spirit of place is to create a simple altar in our home.**

chi-paths in your home

Get to know the energetic anatomy of your space as intimately as you can.

If there are any chi-paths present, find them with your L-rods and track them through the room, then on through the house and outside – you will want to track these all the way from where they enter your property to where they leave. Find out their polarity and intensity, their state of peace or trauma, and how they affect the human health aura.

Notice the health of any plants that you find on the chi path, and whether it runs under beds or chairs or through places where animals sleep. It is best not to spend prolonged periods sitting or standing directly in chi-paths, particularly if they are of a strong yin nature.

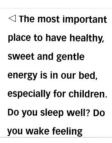

◁ **The most important place to have healthy, sweet and gentle energy is in our bed, especially for children. Do you sleep well? Do you wake feeling refreshed?**

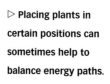

▷ **Placing plants in certain positions can sometimes help to balance energy paths.**

△ **Rooms that work well in a house tend to have a good match of their energy to their function. Rooms where the energy field is incongruous to the use of space feel awkward and difficult.**

energy fields to activities

Different energy fields are appropriate for different human activities. During sleep for example, it is most appropriate to be in a serene, very gentle and moderate energy field, without any strong or highly polarized chi. Ideally our bed is placed where only the tiny capillary lines of chi feed a constant and gentle energy to us. The bed and bedroom generally should be kept in a state of energetic clarity and cleanliness. Healing any etheric traumas and clearing the space of disturbed memory is important before you start using a room as your bedroom. You may also want to clear and balance the energy after an argument or any period of illness, or if your dreams seem troubled and tense.

If you routinely sleep heavily and wake unrefreshed you should dowse carefully to ensure that there is not an excess of yin chi running through your bed.

If you do find energetic problems in your bedroom, apply the healing techniques that we have learned. Ask for the help and co-operation of the spirit of place to ease and repattern the energy flow and create a safe and nurturing space for you at every level. Our sleeping position is the most important environmental factor for our sustained health.

high energy areas

You may find one or more power spots in your home of varying magnitude. These are ideal areas for any creative activity, whether cooking, writing, painting, doing healing work or other spiritual practices. It is best to limit your time in intense power-centres and it is very important to keep them clean and clear, because they hold and amplify thoughts and emotions. They are very useful, but should not be neglected.

Cleaning and clearing a space can be as simple as asking the spirit of place to heal and balance all the energies there, or you may need to use one or more tools such as bells, candles, incense and so on to raise enough focused intention to restore health.

Your dowsing will guide you as to whether peace and balance are present, and if not what you need to do to restore it.

Begin a practice of dialogue with the spirit of your home and of monitoring the energies present.

Pay attention to your imagination and your intuitive feelings as well as your dowsing. Observe the energy changes that follow the daily, monthly and yearly cycles. You will find this increased awareness both revealing and richly rewarding.

▽ **Becoming intimate with the spirit and energy of your home will greatly deepen your relationship with the space. Be sure to keep high-use areas energetically clear and well balanced.**

The spirit of work

The energy fields most suitable for work depend on the nature of the work itself. The standard Chinese formula for human activity space is for there to be a relationship between yang and yin chi, in a 3:2 ratio respectively. This gives us exposure to both polarities but gives us a slightly expansive energy overall. However, some tasks are best performed in a very serene environment, and others require a higher level of intense, inspirational energy.

When assessing work space, first meet and greet the spirit of place. Next dowse generally to discover the nature, quality and health of the energy field overall, and then dowse further, area by area, to become intimately familiar with the energetic anatomy of the etheric field.

Ideally, match the functional use of the space to the energy field present or, if this is not possible, ask the spirit of place that the field be repatterned to support your activities there. Perform any healing or clearing for the space as necessary.

geopathic stress at work

One very important consideration for a business is to ascertain whether the overall energy field of the business premises are well matched to the basic nature of the business, that is, whether the spirit of your enterprise is compatible with the spirit of that place.

If your business is three-years-old or more and is thriving in its current location, then the answer to this question is almost certainly "Yes". If it is less than three-years-old or is not thriving, then your dowsing may hold the key to the long-term success or failure of your enterprise.

Business premises that are geopathically stressed or that carry significantly traumatized place memory will often have a rapid turnover of business occupants. A new business will move in, fail to thrive, and either fail altogether or soon move out. The next business is likely to have a similar fate.

One of the core understandings and observations of working with the energy field of place is that any given place, in the absence of focused energetic intervention, will exhibit a repeating pattern in the lives and health of sequential occupants or residents. This applies to all places, whether commercial, public or domestic.

◁ **Dowsing for geopathic stress in the workplace is important as it can have devastating effects on the dynamics between members of staff, and the success of the business itself. L-rods or a pendulum can be used to locate it.**

◁ **Those living and working close to the land have a relationship with place that is profound, yet simple and matter of fact, and goes far beyond words.**

In a business environment, signs that there is geopathic stress or traumatic place memory include a high sickness rate, poor communication between employees and management, poor concentration, low creativity, low productivity, lethargy and depression. Members of the public may intuitively avoid coming into a stressed retail space, and there are often problems with goods assembled in a stressed manufacturing location. Geopathic stress in an office space has a direct impact on the performance and health of those working there.

Planting a business in an energy field is similar to planting a flower in the garden. To thrive it will need the right kind of nurturing conditions. If you are looking for new business premises, either to start a new business or to expand an existing one, take your pendulum and L-rods with you when you go to look at the prospective site.

Greet the spirit of place there and let it know who you are and what your business intentions are.

Ask if this is a location where your business would be welcome and nurtured and would thrive. Phrase your questions carefully and pay close attention to the answers.

A straight "No" should send you looking elsewhere. A "Yes, but ..." or a "No, but ..." answer may suggest that healing or repatterning is required or that the location might offer itself for something different than you had originally intended. Allow the spirit of place to offer you its insight and inspiration. Check any ideas that you might get with your dowsing.

Of course a straight "Yes" speaks for itself. If you have several locations to choose from, you can ask: "Is this the best location for my business?". Time spent dowsing before committing to new projects is time well invested.

matching tasks to locations

In an established work location, where the spirit is supportive and the energy fields balanced, harmonious and clean, the main consideration is of matching tasks to relevant locations.

Tasks that involve long periods in one place, that require sustained focus or attention to detail or that involve operating dangerous machinery should be performed where the energy field is very serene, well-balanced and even. One does not want strongly polarized or locally intense chi or chi-paths in such places or for such tasks.

Tasks that require relatively short, unsustained bursts of creativity or inspiration will be well supported by yang chi-paths and power-centres.

Yin-chi locations should be avoided other than for brief periods of introspection and grounding or for letting go of intense emotional energy. Both mechanical and

◁ When the energy field of a place is balanced and harmonious, creative work tends to go smoothly.

electrical equipment are more likely to fail or give trouble if they are in a yin-chi location.

Finally, consider making major decisions on the largest power-centre available, assuming that it is clean and harmonious. This is the location where you can receive the most clear guidance and support from the tutelary spirit, where your intuition will be most powerfully engaged and where your intentions will carry their best energy.

When applying spiritual technologies in the workplace, be impeccably clean, honest and ethical in everything that you do. Maintain the highest personal integrity and

do not try to use your powers to win at another's expense. Rather, see your efforts as being for the highest good of all concerned, not only yourself, but your employees, employers and clients. When we engage at the level of spirit, we are truly held to account.

This is not to discourage you from using your dowsing at work. Quite the opposite, as with our relationship with the landscape, it is time for us to reclaim the sacred nature of work in our lives. For a human to be fully healthy, their work must be a loving and joyful act of self-expression, no matter how simple. Work becomes more creative and fun this way and less of a routine chore.

◁ Those locations where we spend the most time are the most important to check and balance carefully.

▷ Power centres are ideal for supporting intense, focused, high energy tasks, and can greatly enhance collaboration and communication. Hospitals should be centred on an appropriate power centre.

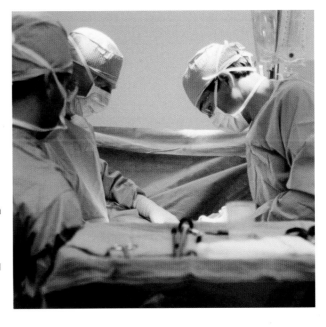

Dowsing in the garden

Dowsing is of immense use in the garden. It allows us to communicate with the spirit of place, and also with nature spirits including those of elemental and devic consciousness who are directly concerned with plant growth. This gives an added depth of spiritual experience and connection for anyone who loves to have their fingers in soil.

We can trace chi-paths through the garden and identify any power-centres present, allowing us to organize our use of the space in synergy with the natural pattern.

Dowsing can help us to select the most appropriate species to plant in any location, and also to bring plants into a space to enhance its energy field with their presence.

devic and elemental spirits

The overall growth and vitality of plant life is the domain of nature spirits called devas. These spirits will help and guide us in every part of our relationship with plants and will act both as our gardening allies and tutors.

Using the power of your imagination, you can dialogue with the devic spirits in your garden. However it may be easier for you to communicate with them initially if you can find a power-centre to help increase levels of sensitivity and awareness.

◁ **Devic spirits guide the overall growth and vitality of plants.**

Centre and clear yourself, and visualize yourself in a column of golden light. Check your "Yes" signal. Introduce yourself and state your intentions: "I am (name) and this is my garden. I would like to grow beautiful flowers here and also fruit and vegetables to feed my family. I wish to communicate with the principal deva of this garden. Is this timely and appropriate?"

If "Yes", ask: "Is communication easier if I am in one particular location?" It may be that it doesn't matter where in the garden you are, however if this does matter, use an L-rod in an outstretched arm and slowly turn your body around in a circle while asking: "Show me the direction to go to communicate most easily with the principal deva here."

When the rod sticks in one direction, walk that way with both of your L-rods in search position, asking for the exact spot until your get your "Here it is!" response.

Let yourself become still and quiet, and then openly share with the deva all your thoughts and fantasies about the garden. Through a process of dialogue using the power of your imagination and by checking specific points with "Yes/No" dowsing, see if you can find a synergistic, co-creative strategy for planting and managing the space in collaboration with the devic spirit.

Check out thoughts of which species will do well and in which locations, and whether a rotational sequence or other crops are needed to replenish soil fertility.

Once you have an overall idea and plan, you may wish to "take a walk with the deva" and go around the garden, dowsing different areas to see if your ideas and current management are at their best or could be improved. It may take a little time but it will be worth it.

◁ **By entering into a co-creative dialogue, gardening becomes an immensely rich and personal interaction with spirit.**

soils, seeds and seedlings

Dowsing is a valuable tool in helping us assess the overall necessity and specific requirements for soil amendments in our garden in a particular spot or even for an individual plant.

This can be done by dowsing at the spot, or else back in the kitchen with a soil sample, or even over a gardening catalogue. "Does the rose bed in the west corner need manure this season? Does it need any phosphate? Would this brand be best? Or this brand?"

You can also dowse to pick seeds out of a catalogue using your dowsing. "Would this kind of tomato do well here? Would this kind do better?" You can also dowse over the seed-packets to find the exact spot to plant them in.

If you have brought a new plant into your garden, it is likely to thrive best if planted somewhere that it likes. You can dowse for its best location, for any soil amendments that it needs, even for its orientation. "Round to the right a little further? Further still?" You can use your dowsing to help you keep an eye on it while it re-establishes itself in its new location. "Is it getting enough water? Too much?" This can be helpful with species that are difficult to grow or that are at the edge of their climate tolerance, or that have not arrived in your garden in the best of health.

△ **Laying out a garden with reference to the spirit of place and to the underlying pattern of subtle energies, greatly enhances the health and beauty of the space.**

chi-paths and power-centres

As with your home and work space, find out as much as you can about the etheric, emotional and mental energy fields of your garden. Perform any necessary healing and clearing work, and ask the deva whether etheric repatterning would be helpful and appropriate to support the garden overall. Not only will plants grow better when the energies are clean, clear, balanced and harmonious, but you will also attract many more birds and other wildlife into your garden if the energy is sweet. Furthermore, it will make the garden much more friendly for you, and greatly increase the vitality of any food that you grow.

Finally, bear in mind that different species have different preferences and consider the pattern of chi-paths and the chi preferences for each. The list below is very limited – you will learn most by dowsing and observing your own garden. Plants grown where they are not supported by the available chi will be weak and stunted, prone to disease and frost, and generally less healthy.

Everything that lives in your compost heap and helps create it would love to be over crossing yin chi-paths. Bees also like to live over crossing yin chi-paths, they will be happier and make more honey if you place their hive where your dowsing shows.

▷ **Dowsing helps us to choose specific places where trees and plants will thrive. It also helps to balance the energies around existing plantings.**

PLANT CHI PREFERENCES

Use this list as a starting point for discovering the chi preferences for different species. You can then dowse plants from your own garden to find out their preferences, and compile your own list.

Yin chi-lovers	Yin chi-avoiders
beans	beech
larch	Brussels sprouts
medicinal herbs	cauliflower
oak	cucumber
sycamore	elm
tomatoes	fruit trees
ivy	lime
	peas

Energy and *power centres*

A power-centre is a point in the earth's etheric web where yin and yang chi are both present. The effect of bringing these polar opposite, elemental forces together is to create a synergistic union where the energetic outcome is greater than that which either the yin or the yang energy can achieve on its own. It is exactly the same energetic fusion that allows the creation of new life through sexual union.

To place ourselves in the energy field of these nodal points is to put ourselves in a profoundly creative space.

There are many consequences of this. One of these is that a very deep form of healing and renewal becomes available to us. Because the full spectrum of yin and yang energy is present, we can draw on any part of that spectrum to replenish stressed and depleted parts of our own energy field. Also, our subtle body is exposed to a larger, more powerful energy field that is whole and irrepressibly creative, and we can draw on this potential energy to heal and recreate any parts of ourselves that have become damaged or dysfunctional.

Power-centres are also the points in the landscape where the etheric, emotional and mental energies are most intensely present. This means that at these points all qualities of spirit are more available to us, if we can open ourselves up to them.

◁ **Power centres have immense capacity to inspire and transform. They offer themselves as spiritual doorways, and as nodal points for perceiving and influencing the wider landscape around them.**

▽ **Spiritual power long outlives the cycles of politics and economics that ebb and flow throughout time. The spirit of place has its own cycles of time. Rhythmically and periodically it may call people to it, perhaps as pilgrims, while at other times it may enter a very quiet or dormant period.**

health and balance

Owing to the intensity of their vibrational field, power-centres hold memory and information more than other parts of the energetic web, and their influence is greater upon us than when we are at other points on the web. It is therefore very important to keep power-centres clean and balanced.

Our relationship with them depends upon their size and intensity and how prepared we are to encounter them. We may enjoy the experience of paddling in the lapping waves on a beach, or if we raise our energy to match the power of larger waves, we may have the thrilling experience of playing in big surf. The bigger the surf, the greater the energy in the field, and the more prepared, focused and more energetic we need to be to hold our balance.

When we engage with power-centres our own preparation and balance is therefore important. Whatever consciousness we

▷ **The greatness of the spirit of a place may be reflected in the excellence of the architecture that it inspires.**

hold when we enter a power-centre will be mirrored back to us and also projected into the surrounding energy field. If we are not in very good balance and enter a very large energy field, our own emotional or intellectual state may be magnified to a level that we find intensely uncomfortable.

Paradoxically, both healing and chaos can occur in power-centres. Which of these we will experience depends on the magnitude and balance of the power-centre itself and the balance of our own inner energies. However, it is also the case that healing and inspiration can come to us through chaos.

△ **Where elemental forces are strong and intense – even overpowering – mindfulness and clarity are essential for keeping us centred and balanced.**

POWER-CENTRE PRACTICE

• Let the power-centre become a place that you regularly visit, each time checking if it needs healing or balancing.

• Ask when you visit whether it is appropriate for you to be there at that particular time, sometimes it may need to be left to itself, and it might be better to return another day.

• If you have any spiritual practice, such as meditation, yoga or T'ai Chi, bring that to the power-centre. Even if you only visit and sit and use your imagination to open a dialogue with the spirit of the power-centre, you will find that gradually your focus and clarity improve, your energies become strengthened, and your balance easier to hold.

• Communing regularly with a nodal point on the web also powerfully attunes us with the rhythm and cycles of the earth, helping us to move with much more ease and fluidity through life.

• Visit your power-centre at sunrise, at noon, at sunset, at midnight, and get to know all of its moods and sub-personalities, by doing this, we come to know ourselves.

cultivating a relationship

As we become increasingly aware of subtle energy, it is appropriate to cultivate a relationship with a power-centre. Ideally, this occurs at two levels. The first level is to work with a power-centre in our own space. Whether large or small, there will be a yin/yang intersection in almost any place, and if there is not, you can call on the spirit of place to bring one. The second level at which to engage with power-centres is in the wider landscape where we can have access to larger energy fields at the community level.

Clear and centre yourself, visualize yourself in a column of golden light, and check your "Yes" response. State: "I wish to dowse about power-centres. Is this timely and appropriate?" If "Yes", ask: "Is there a power-centre in this space that it would be good and healthy for me to be working with at this time?"

If the answer is "Yes", use your directional dowsing technique to guide you to its location. Typically it will be experienced as an enchanted place, and you may well know already where it is.

Once you have identified the power-centre that you will be working with, take some time to greet the spirit there, and ask if it needs any healing, clearing or repatterning to come into its most whole and balanced state. Support it with your love and healing energy as it does this. Dowse with your L-rods to become intimate with the pattern and characteristics of the chi there.

The geomantic landscape

Geomancy is the name given to the practice of reading and relating to the subtle energies of the earth.

It is a core part of the relationship that all cultures have had with the environment and is intimately woven into the cultural fabric of indigenous people everywhere, be they Celt or Sami, !Kung or Inuit, Australian aboriginal or native American. The geomantic awareness of all these people is codified and held slightly differently depending on their own social, political and economic structure. Geomancy faded in western European culture at the time of the Protestant Reformation, when the mass consciousness was changing, facilitating the subsequent rise of rationalism and industrialism. Today, Feng Shui, the Chinese code of geomancy stemming from the imperial culture of China, is currently becoming popularized and widely studied in the west.

To both orientate themselves in their landscape and to connect in the most powerful and life-affirming way with the ever changing, pulsing energies of spirit, all cultures have sought out and engaged in

GEOMANCY
All forms of geomancy have the following three things in common.

- An awareness of the presence and influence of the dragon energies of the earth.
- An awareness of the presence and influence of the cyclical, celestial energies of the heavenly bodies.
- A recognition of the world of shape, pattern and form which is moved and guided by the first two.

Magical cultures have referred to these as the upper, middle and lower worlds. Human beings live in the middle world, and we are influenced by the dragon energies of the lower and the planetary influences of the upper world. Or to put it another way, by the movement of energy in time and space.

intimate relationships with power-centres. In exactly the same way that communing with a power-centre in our garden connects us to the spirit of our home, the larger nodal points around us are places where the community can connect with the greater spirit of the land.

Power-centres are points of contact, and can function rather like umbilical cords, feeding and nourishing the spirit of an individual, of a community or even of an entire culture, depending on their magnitude.

In exactly the same way that we become allied with and are under the tutelage of the spirit of place in our home, so a nation becomes identified with and characterized

△ **Communities and cultures define themselves in reference to a particular place, rather like an umbilical point in their landscape. The path to it may often look like an umbilical cord.**

by the spirit of the major power-centre that they claim as their point of reference, such as their capital city or most holy shrine.

acts of pilgrimage

It is for this reason that we not only need to develop an intimate relationship with our own personal power-centre, but we also need to develop a relationship with the larger power-centres in the landscape occupied by our community.

Spending time in such places helps to attune us to the spirit of the wider landscape which holds, supports and meets the needs of our community. For the community to be healthy and sustaining, we all need to be in dialogue with the principal tutelary spirit of the landscape. This will guide us in how to form the right relationship with the seen and unseen forces that ultimately act to restore balance to all living systems.

The act of pilgrimage has long been held as a spiritual journey to the holy places – the recognized power-centres – of the culture. Visiting these places was believed to offer a transformational journey of inspiration and

healing at a deeply spiritual level. A return to the spiritual centre or focal point of the culture was to meet with its most powerful and enlightening spirits.

In many respects it does not matter what we do when we get there, it is simply the going and being present that is the key to the experience. To place our own subtle body in the intensified, healing, balancing and uplifting energy field of a major power-centre is enough.

relationship with the land

Many power-centres are known and marked. You will find them in churches and cathedrals. You will find them in stone circles, in medicine wheels, in kivas, in labyrinths, on sacred mountains and caves, at holy wells, temples and shrines.

Some of them are not marked, however. The energies of the earth shift and repattern from time to time, and it is a while since the power-centres have been publicly explored and acknowledged in some places.

Issues of both environmental and personal health make healing our relationship with the spirit of the land vitally important at this stage in our evolution. We can do this in two ways. We need to engage in healing activities at power-centres, both old and new. This will help to clear them of the accumulated emotional, mental and psychic trauma that

they have witnessed, and to help to ease, balance and restore the flow of chi in their dragons. The second way is by visiting them regularly, in a joyful and celebratory fashion, whether to sing, dance or meditate, to be healed, or spiritually transformed, or to have picnics and fly kites with our children. Simply we need to be there, and to steep ourselves in the wellspring of their nurturing, balancing, healing energy field.

Whichever route you take, don't forget to take your pendulum. Use it to find your spot where you can simply sit and be.

△ Experiencing the subtle body of stones is a way to open us to the spirit of the landscape.

▽ By visiting and witnessing the outer cycles of the landscape throughout the year, we become more attuned to the inner cycles of our own life.

Dowsing
Deeper

The hand moves

And the fire's whirling

Takes different shapes

All things change when we do –

The first word

"-Ah-"

Blossoms into all others

Each of them is true

Kookai, 5th-century Zen master

Dowsing and water-witching

We have learned in this book to dowse with a focus on our health. This is one of the most powerful and useful applications for dowsing, and one in which, by our personal experience of its results, we can gain confidence in our abilities as dowsers, in the validity of dowsing as a technique, and of the power of following the wisdom of our spirit to guide us in our lives. While dowsing for health is of immense value however, it is not its only use.

There is simply no limit to the potential uses of dowsing. We are limited only by our ability to ask clear, concise questions with "Yes/No" answers, by our ability to remain engaged but unattached to the responses that we receive, and, apparently, by the authentic need for us to know the answer to the question that we have asked.

water-witching

In many communities, dowsing (or divining as it is also called) is best known as a means of finding drinking water that can be reached by digging or drilling a well. In some places, water dowsers are known as water witches. Dowsing for water is an immensely valuable and practical application of the art. Competent water dowsers can identify not only the exact location of

water in the earth, but also accurately predict its depth below the surface, its flow rate in litres/gallons per minute or per hour, and its drinkable quality. Some water dowsers are 100 per cent consistent in their accuracy.

Dowsing for water is a natural ability that all humans have. The ability to find water in survival situations has embedded this capability deep in our psyche.

To dowse for water, we must first establish our water needs. Those of a single home are

△ **Before the widespread piping and pumping of water, every farm and isolated dwelling needed its own well or spring. Water dowsing has always been an essential part of rural life.**

less than for a farm or factory, so the daily volume of water required must be decided. Approximately 23 litres/5 gallons per minute is considered a plentiful supply at adequate pressure for a normal, single domestic residence.

When dowsing for water, as for anything else, we need to be as specific and focused as we can be with our questions. Let us assume that we are searching for water for a home:

First clear and centre yourself, and visualize yourself in a column of golden light. State: "I want to dowse for water for this home". Check your "Yes" response.

Ask: "Is this timely and appropriate?" If "Yes", state: "I need to find a source of good, pure, uncontaminated water, healthy for humans to drink, that will give a recoverable volume of 23 litres/5 gallons per minute, all year" or whatever your requirements are.

◁ **To help you tune in, you could imagine the water of a stream flowing around your hands.**

◁ **Having clearly defined the quality and quantity of water that we need, we can begin dowsing to locate the whereabouts of a suitable source.**

worthy, whether the avocado will be ripe in time for Saturday dinner, even how many people will turn up for a party. The uses of dowsing are innumerable and only limited by your own imagination.

Let your dowsing be a friend. Treat it with respect, use it for reasonable and genuine need, and always check your answers with your common sense.

Then ask: "Is such a supply available on this piece of land?" You will need to predetermine where you may look (this will normally be dictated by property ownership).

If the answer to this question is "No", continue dowsing until you discover what is available, perhaps there is a source of good water at 14 litres/3 gallons per minute, and you can accommodate your needs with a smaller volume by establishing a holding tank of a certain size.

If the answer is "Yes", ask: "Is there more than one source of such water?" If there is, you will want to determine which is the best source.

Considerations as to what constitutes the best source include the depth of the water (drilling further costs more and may require a more powerful pump) the volume available (if other houses are built nearby it will be good to have a productive well to share), the distance of the water from the house, and the drinkable quality (water is such a key part of our health and dietary needs that we might choose as a priority to drill for the very best, most health-giving water). There may also be local considerations of site practicality and access.

Identify which of the available sources best meets your needs with "Yes/No" dowsing questions. (You can also simply allow the wisdom of your spirit to guide you, asking to be shown the best source of water for a well, given all things known and unknown at this time.)

dowsing for everything

Traditionally, and even now, dowsing is used for the location of minerals and oil. It has been applied in many military operations and has applications too useful to be dismissed as unconventional nonsense. Rescue teams as well as numerous police forces call on the services of dowsers to aid in search and recovery efforts. Construction crews routinely dowse to locate site utilities, and farmers dowse to find blocked or lost field drains.

You can dowse to see whether the cake is perfectly baked, whether the plant needs to be watered, whether one used car will be more reliable than another, whether the trouble is the carburettor or a spark plug, whether your client is genuinely credit

△ **L-rods are probably the most popular and widely used tools for water dowsing.**

▽ **Dowsing can be used for anything – even checking whether the cake or soufflé is cooked or not.**

Further dowsing

Cultivating the dowser inside us is a process of gaining self-confidence and trust in the wisdom of our spirit, leading to a deep acceptance of our true self. It can become a vehicle for a powerful, self-led spiritual journey offering a personal channel for dialogue with the divine. Because of its power as a tool for independent spiritual growth, for hundreds of years dowsing was outlawed by religious institutions who sought to control the spiritual direction of the community.

We now have the freedom to seek spiritually as we choose, but we should exercise caution if using dowsing purely as a tool for spiritual exploration and growth.

All dowsing falls broadly into two categories. The first is that of "tangible target" dowsing, such as dowsing for missing objects, water, faults in car engines – things that have material substance and confirm our dowsing when we find them. The second category is "intangible target" dowsing, such as dowsing for issues that can only be confirmed indirectly or subjectively. Spiritual dowsing falls

◁ **Dowsing offers itself as a path of personal spiritual pilgrimage, safely guided by the open heart and open mind.**

into this category. We can sometimes become a little ungrounded and unbalanced if we only use our dowsing for intangible targets . Balance between the two is the key.

responsible dowsing

Keep some of your dowsing practice in the realm of tangible target dowsing. This helps to "ground" your dowsing and to relate the spiritual reality to the physical. If we engage exclusively in intangible target dowsing, it can sometimes develop a quality of escapism that is unhelpful to us and can become a life avoidance technique.

Human beings are blessed with free-will, and the information that we receive through our dowsing will help to inform and guide us in any given situation. Using dowsing in this way is empowering. By contrast, it can sometimes be tempting to ask our dowsing what we should do when we feel overwhelmed or don't want to be responsible for making a difficult decision. Using dowsing to make a decision for us is disempowering. Instead, use your dowsing to inform and empower you so that you can make a clear decision for yourself.

A good check on whether our relationship with dowsing is healthy is to ask ourselves whether it is supporting and affirming our life , our capacity and responsibility for free will. If it is, all is well.

DOWSING ETHICS

There are many things that can be said about dowsing ethics, but there are a few principles that will support us in most situations.

• Dowsing is a personal tool. It gives you direct access to your spirit through your intuition and the language that you choose. This helps you to both perceive and define reality – but only for yourself. Every person is unique so you must be careful not to assume that because something is true for you that it is true for someone else.

• We all have our individual experience of spirit, which reveals itself to us in a form that we can each relate to. Please be careful not to impose beliefs that seem true to you upon others. Instead, share your discoveries and invite others to dowse for themselves. It's far healthier.

• Be careful not to engage in "psychic trespass" through your dowsing. It is possible to use dowsing to discover things about other people and their concerns that they would prefer you did not know – private and confidential matters. To trespass in this way is thought to incur negative spiritual consequences, and in any case, it is not a respectful use of your dowsing.

• As a guiding rule, use your dowsing for those matters which are of genuine and reasonable concern to you personally or to others who have requested your help. Very occasionally, you may have to decide whether dowsing that appears to be in the overwhelming public interest justifies an intrusion upon another's privacy. Always dowse with integrity and you will not go far wrong.

▷ The technique of map dowsing can save a lot of time. Using a map allows you to dowse a large area quickly and with a large scale map it can be surprisingly accurate.

locational dowsing

A further level of skill that we can develop is that of map dowsing. When dowsing on a map, we treat the map as if it were the ground itself, and as though we had a bird's eye view.

If searching for a lost object or missing person, or searching for the best place to site a well or a home or a sanctuary on a very large piece of land, or perhaps when tracing a dragon path across miles of open country, dowsing from a map will make our task much easier and is more practical than site dowsing in the first instance.

There are many techniques and adaptations of techniques for map dowsing. Here are two.

The corner pendulum technique uses the pendulum to indicate a line of direction rather as we have been using an L-rod.

Hold your pendulum over one corner of the map, swinging parallel with one edge.

Ask for it to point towards the object of your search. Its swing will move round until it is swinging straight backwards and forwards, but now pointing in a direction that will lead you over the map.

Follow this line with the pendulum itself or with a finger moving over the map until the pendulum changes its motion into your "Yes" signal. This marks your spot.

Confirm it by dowsing in from another corner for accuracy.

If you are map-dowsing for a linear or sinuous feature such as a dragon path, ask your dowsing to indicate points along the path and then join up the dots.

The second technique is using a ruler. Let us assume we are looking for a single point – perhaps the location of a lost object that could be anywhere over a large area on a map.

Prepare to dowse in the usual way, and when you are attuned and focused, lay the map out flat and take a ruler or straight edge and lay it on the map at one side, and parallel with the edge.

Start your pendulum swinging in neutral. Ask "Please indicate when the ruler is at the location of the (name of object)." Move the ruler slowly over the map, keeping it parallel with one edge of the map.

When your pendulum swings into its "Yes" response, draw a pencil line down the ruler's edge.

Now repeat this with the ruler parallel to the other edge of the map, at 90° to its previous orientation.

Again, when your pendulum indicates that you have arrived at the spot, stop and draw a pencil line along the ruler's edge. Where the two lines cross shows the spot that you are looking for.

In addition to direction finding on a map, there is also a site-dowsing technique for a pendulum, which is an adaptation of the L-rod method and is useful to know.

Simply hold your pendulum in its neutral swing and ask it to show you in which direction the target is, point with your free hand or arm and slowly turn around until your pendulum swings into a "Yes" response. Walk in that direction and ask it to indicate the point you need to know about.

deviceless dowsing

We have been learning to dowse using a pendulum and L-rods. However, dowsing is an internal process, relying ultimately on a particular state of mind and consciousness, and not on any external tools or devices. Once we have built up sufficient experience, we can begin to dowse "deviceless", that is, without using any tools. To do this, you may experiment by visualizing a pendulum or L-rods in your mind's eye as you ask your dowsing question, and watch the response of your visualized tool.

Another technique used when searching for something on the ground, such as a water vein or energy path or a lost object, is to ask the dowsing question, "Show me the location of the ring that my sister has lost" and then scan the ground with your eyes in soft focus until they seem to "stick" or repeatedly return to one spot. This should be the location that you seek. You may also scan an area with your hands and pay attention to changes in temperature or tingling sensations that you experience. Many dowsers use their whole body for deviceless dowsing, and experience a physical and mental relaxation, peace and ease as their "Yes" response and a stiffening and tensing experience to indicate "No". These responses are all highly individual. Explore what works best for you.

△ With practice and experience, we become able to dowse without tools, and use the natural sensitivity of our body to perceive intuitive information.

Fostering the inner healer

Some people have a gift for music. They are naturally inclined towards musicianship and may be exceptionally talented. Their gift can be channelled and focused and their abilities refined through learned skills and techniques. Even without training their ear for rhythm and melody and their passion for expressing themselves through music will bring pleasure both to themselves and to those around them. However, in the absence of self-consciousness, every single one of us can make a joyful noise and carry a tune to our own personal satisfaction, if not to the standard needed for a concert performance.

Healing gifts are similar to those for music. The gift of healing is held to be one of the gifts of the spirit, present in the very essence of who we truly are, and is not something learned or acquired.

In the core of our being, we can all heal powerfully and effectively and have a deep intuitive knowledge of how to do this. We may not think that we know how to heal, or even have any idea of how to go about it until we start, but if our intention is to heal and we allow our naturally wise and intuitive spirit self to take over, then the healing energy will flow and healing will occur.

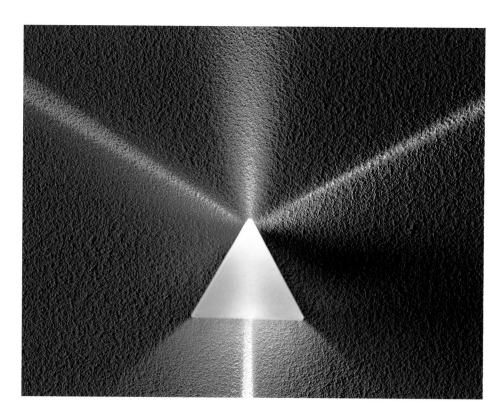

The capacity for healing then, both for self-healing and for healing others, is a fundamental and inevitably present part of the human spirit. Certainly some of those among us are more naturally inclined to express themselves through a vocation in healing, and indeed may have extraordinary talents and abilities. However, as with music, we can also learn skills and tools, techniques and modalities, for focusing, channelling and refining our natural healing abilities for the good of others and ourselves.

approaching life with a healing attitude

One of the greatest spiritual truths is that whatever we focus our attention upon, we give power to and attract into our lives. In this way we can cultivate and encourage our inner healer by continually, but gently developing attitudes of mind that make more space for healing and the healer to show up in our lives.

△ **Divine energy of love and healing is unlimited. We need only open ourselves to receiving and channelling it, and focus our attention on wholeness and health.**

Many of us have learned to be effective in life by becoming problem-solvers. We approach any new situation asking the question, "Now what's the problem here?" We address any problem or dilemma by looking for the pathology, the thing that's not working, that needs to be fixed or replaced or removed altogether.

While this is successful as a problem-solving method, it trains us to be constantly looking for pathology and dysfunction and, lo and behold, the spiritual truth holds good, and more and more pathology and dysfunction shows up in our lives for us to address. We attract it by looking for it.

All of the same situations can be equally effectively addressed by asking a different question: "How can I heal this? What does this situation need to make it whole, to make it work properly, and to restore peace and balance to it?"

◁ **The small flame of an individual human spirit is of the same essence as the divine fire.**

The final outcome of both approaches may be similar, but the process that we have engaged in and the quality of energy that we have channelled is quite different.

In one approach we have acted as a fault-finding, trouble-shooting, diagnostician. In the other we have acted as peace-bringer, restorer of balance and a healer.

How this affects our experience of the world is profound. Try it and feel how very different your daily experience of the world becomes. To cultivate a healing attitude is to cultivate compassion and grace.

meditating on health

As well as focusing our intellectual energies on healing, we can also nurture those same qualities at their source in spirit. A simple self-healing meditation is of immense benefit and value, not only for enhancing our own health but also for strengthening our own healing capacity which can then be used to help others.

The following meditation will greatly nurture your inner healer, changing the way that people relate to you, and how you relate to your life.

Sit quietly with a relaxed, erect spine. Pay attention to your breathing without trying to control it, and visualize yourself in a column of light.

Visualize and become aware of the flame of your spirit dancing in your heart. Imagine it there as a bright flame like that of a candle, only much more vivid and intense, a fire burning in your heart and vitalizing the centre of your humanity.

Now let your attention move, scanning through your body, your emotions and your mind. Find any areas of tension, be they physical, emotional or mental. Using your imagination, take the tense, stored energy from those places, leaving them relaxed and full of ease, the energy flowing gently and harmoniously through them.

Take the blocked energy, and gently and lovingly place it into the fire. Watch as it burns and disappears, the energy is still present within you, but is now transformed. Ask that it be transformed into an energy of truth and beauty.

Continue placing any tense, dark, stuck, angry or fearful energy into the fire of your spirit, repeatedly asking that it be transformed into truth and beauty. When you are fully relaxed and at peace you are complete.

▽ **Self healing, and maintaining our personal centre and balance, requires focus and patience. Wholeness must be first located inside ourselves in order to then manifest it in our external life.**

The movement of energy in time and space

We live in a culture that relates to time as something linear. This is in contrast to the relationship with time held by primal cultures living much more intimately with their landscape than we do with ours. They live in harmony with the ever-repeating changes that move through and govern their lives, as the cycles of each day each month, each season and each year, and make their progress around the wheel, to inevitably return and begin anew that circular journey.

A belief in linearity and unending growth creates a dysfunctional relationship with our energetic environment. It causes us to deny the inevitable nature and fundamental health of the circle. At the most physical level, our current economies are built on the premise of indefinite growth, in progress and expansion. This is not a consciousness that helps the promotion of health.

Cancer is the medical term for a thing that continues to grow without reference to the waxing and waning cycles that influence and regulate those things that surround it.

△ **The spirit of the earth expresses itself in the cycle of the seasons.**

the sacred circle

Many spiritual traditions represent spirit by a circle. It is a map of consciousness, showing how energy moves in time and space. The philosophy can be understood by following the cycle around the wheel of the year.

Follow it round on the diagram. We can start anywhere – let's pick the north.

◁ **By observing the reflection of the outer cycles of nature on the inner cycles of our life – like that of the trees on the water – we perceive our own nature by the patterns we create.**

In the north it is midwinter. This is the point of greatest contraction and introversion. We are most intimate with ourselves and each other.

Now turn to the north-east. An imperceptible expansion is occurring. The ground begins to thaw and the seeds stir in the soil, unseen, and begin to grow.

We arrive in the east and the spring equinox. This is a time of visible expansion and growth, the shoots are above the ground and reaching for the sky.

We come to the south-east, a time of flowering, pollination and fertility.

Now we reach the south and midsummer. Plants are maturing, and the energy is transforming and gathering into seed heads.

We come to the south-west and west, the harvesting first of grain and later of fruit.

At the beginning of November we reach the north-west. Now, the vegetation is dying back, and the energy is returning to the soil. Seeds are sown that will lie dormant until the following spring, gestating.

Our breath is what connects us to life, and like the wheel of the year, it follows a circular pattern, breathing in, and breathing out. Sit quietly and observe your breath as you gently breath in and out for a few moments. You have just experienced the cycle of life.

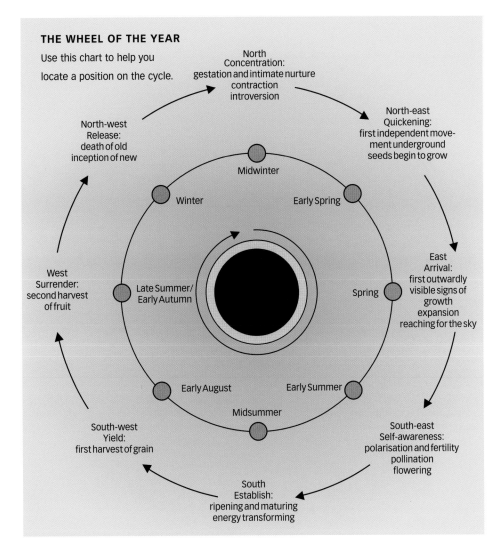

THE WHEEL OF THE YEAR

Use this chart to help you
locate a position on the cycle.

North
Concentration:
gestation and intimate nurture
contraction
introversion

North-east
Quickening:
first independent move-
ment underground
seeds begin to grow

North-west
Release:
death of old
inception of new

Midwinter

Winter

Early Spring

West
Surrender:
second harvest
of fruit

Late Summer/
Early Autumn

Spring

East
Arrival:
first outwardly
visible signs of
growth
expansion
reaching for the sky

Early August

Early Summer

Midsummer

South-west
Yield:
first harvest of grain

South-east
Self-awareness:
polarisation and fertility
pollination
flowering

South
Establish:
ripening and maturing
energy transforming

health is a circle made whole

Everything in our lives inevitably follows a cycle. Some of these cycles are very short, some are much longer. We can learn a tremendous amount by looking to see at what point on the circle any of our different projects or endeavours lie.

For example, any business venture starts with a seed idea, which is planted in the north-west and spends some time digesting inwardly. It then begins to have some life and movement of its own as it progresses to the north-east. It then gathers strength and momentum and appears as an outward form in the east, before moving to the south-east, where it is starting to become established and is attracting other fertilizing energy to it.

Following its cycle it then matures and ripens in the south, and starts to yield its harvest, first in the south-west, and then a second crop in the west. At the end of the cycle in the north-west, the seed, the kernel of wisdom, is returned to the soil once again and is reinvested into the next cycle.

There are many profound images of health. One which is important to understand is seeing how the degenerative, contractive phase is actually a healthy and necessary part of the cycle. It is a time of replenishment which will feed the generative side of the cycle. Death of the old must come before the birth of the new, liberating the energy required for re-investment and recreation. For the cycle of life to continue, the energy must flow freely around it.

If we injure our arm for instance, the first thing we do is to hold it close to our body so that it does not move. Following trauma, movement of an injury is painful, but as healing occurs, motion returns. Trauma limits the free movement of energy. If an injury is not healed, an energetic constriction at that point on the cycle builds up, and energy gets stuck, leaving a scarcity of energy beyond it.

All trauma, whether physical, emotional and/or mental, can be seen in this way, and all healing can be understood in terms of easing and releasing the contracted and stuck energy, allowing it to continue the cycle.

dowsing the circle

This perspective gives us a powerful understanding and insight which can help to support healing in our lives.

Consider any current situation in your life where energy has stopped flowing, where you feel stuck and in need of healing. Try to identify this stuckness as a point on the circle. You may or may not be conscious of the trauma that is responsible. Many of our traumas stem from our childhood and are present as fears or misguided beliefs of personal inadequacy.

Clear and centre yourself, visualizing a column of golden light. Thinking of the particular concern, state: "I wish to know where on the wheel of my life this energy has become traumatized and stuck. Is this timely and appropriate?" If "Yes", place a finger anywhere on the diagram.

Slowly move your finger around the circle as you ask "Where is the trauma in this cycle?" When you reach the place, your pendulum will give you a "Yes" response.

See if you can relate to the nature of the trauma and the energy block indicated, and whether it is helpful to consider it in these terms. There will almost certainly be congested energy in the area of your life relating to the point before the blockage and a lack of energy in the part of the cycle following.

Identifying and understanding energy flow in these terms can give us powerful awareness to focus healing for ourselves. You can begin this process by visualizing the trauma dissolving, and energy starting to move freely around the circle once again.

▽ **The circle maps the movement of energy.
Dowsing shows us where the pulse has reached,
and the location and nature of any trauma.**

The embrace of wholeness

Many of the things that we have explored in this book may seem new and unfamiliar and perhaps a little strange or challenging. We are not generally used to the thought that the answers to our questions and concerns of our life are available to us in the most simple way. We are more familiar with the expectation that guidance in our lives comes from outside of us, from people who seem to know more or appear to see further than us.

Of course, we can draw inspiration and learn enormously from everyone that we meet. Whether they are contemporary or historical figures they may be teachers and role-models for us in particular areas of our lives. However, each one of us is truly unique and the circumstances and details of our lives make it virtually impossible for anyone else to ultimately guide us along our life-path.

△ **Life, like water, is ever-renewing itself, ever-replenishing. In health, we allow ourself to be moved, refreshed and recreated by the ever-moving stream of our life.**

◁ **The embrace of wholeness is as simple as opening ourself to what is already within us.**

incorporating the spirit

The ultimate guiding lights and points of reference for us are almost invariably spiritual ones. However, most of us spend the greatest amount of our energy focused on physical, mental and emotional concerns. How to incorporate the energy and relationship of spirit into our life can be a dilemma for us, an added burden that seems to be in contradiction to the many pressing material concerns that we have to meet. Perhaps the path that reconciles this dilemma is to integrate our sense of the spiritual into every part of our physical, emotional and mental activity.

Spirituality has become associated almost exclusively with religious practice. While it is indeed to be found there, it is not the only way of connecting with our spiritual selves.

Each of us is simultaneously a creature of body, mind and spirit. We are spiritually connected to everything that we think, feel and do. Seen in this light, the spiritual is not a separate part of our lives so much as an intimate, ever-present and interwoven reality. A glorious part of ourselves that can be re-activated and energized.

△ **Meditation strengthens and deepens the connection between body, mind and spirit.**

opening to spirituality

Part of the reason that spirit remains unacknowledged is that we feel overwhelmed by something that we have no personal tools to deal with, or relate to. As with other matters, we have become accustomed to seeking spiritual guidance from outside ourselves, feeling unskilled or even forgetful of how to open the doorway.

Cultivate dowsing in your life. It is a simple but invaluable tool for opening that doorway. It offers each one of us a direct and personal way to interact with, experience the presence of, and seek guidance from spirit. More than this, it allows our own spirit to become a totally present and integrated part of even the most mundane parts of our lives, from gardening and baking to business and healing. It creates a richness, awareness and a great sense of contentment and purpose that people often only dream of.

The more we use dowsing in our lives, the more we strengthen our connection with our spirit and ease and facilitate the dialogue between the different levels of our being. In this way, our outer life becomes increasingly congruent and integral with our inner life. Thoughts, emotions and actions reflect our deepest sense of who we are as individuals, flowing outwards into the world from a secure sense of self-acceptance and self-celebration.

learning to trust

As we trust and integrate the wisdom from our spirit more and more, the channel of information and inspiration deepens and strengthens, and we gradually find that we need to use tools (such as the pendulum, L-rods and others) less and less in our dowsing.

The pendulum, L-rods and other dowsing tools can perhaps be considered as keys to open the door. Once we have opened it often enough, we no longer find that we need to lock it afterwards, or indeed, even to close it at all. We become increasingly secure in a profound sense of inner-knowing or sense of rightness about things which the process of dowsing introduces us to and teaches us familiarity with.

The more we recognize that sense of inner rightness, the more we can dowse without tools. In fact, after a while, we can dowse without even focusing on or thinking about it at all. It then becomes hard to say where dowsing starts or stops. The wisdom of our spirit becomes ever present in a seamless and integrated way, facilitating our every decision and action without us having to consider it as a distinct and separate activity. This process is a gentle and gradual one, and evolves at its own speed and in its own way, without our having to worry or coax it along. The more we can relax with our dowsing and what it brings us, the more likely this is to occur.

With this unfolding of spiritual integration, the promise of original health will be fulfilled for you. You will find yourself naturally and intuitively choosing to do what your body needs to be healthy, choosing to engage with what your mind needs for stimulation and satisfaction, and finding yourself celebrating in the self-expression and fulfilment of your spirit's purpose.

▽ **Just as this well cover is a doorway to the waters within, so too is there a doorway to the spiritual world in nature. "The breeze at dawn has secrets to tell you – don't go back to sleep."**

Index and Acknowledgements

absent healing 52-3
acupuncture 58
allergies 30-31
auras 45,64,74

chakra system 45
chi 56,58,59,61,64-6,68,70,74,78,79
cycle of life 92,93

desensitization 30,31
devas 36,37,78,79
diet 25-9
directional dowsing 63,65
dowsing
    basic dowsing responses 15
    basic principles 12
    blind 21
    ethics 88
    exercises 16-17
    locational 89
    preparation 14
    responses 18-19
    responsible 88
    the sequence 20-21
dragons 58-9,63-5

elements, the 69
empowerment basics 24
energy
    awareness 60-61
    fields 75,77,81,83
    lines 59
engaged non-attachment 16,20
essential (aromatic) oils 32-3,69

flower essences and remedies 34-5,36-7,69

garden, dowsing in the 78-9
geomancy 82
geopathic stress 61,66-8,76-7

healing gift, the 42-3,90-91
health 10,24,25,91
herbalism 34
holding patterns 48
home, the spirit of a 74-5

imagination 73,75,78,87
immune system 30,31,66
intangible target dowsing 88

L-rod, the 62-3,65
landscape, the geomanic 82-3
ley lines 59

medicine wheels 83
minerals 12,26,28-9,87

pendulum
    basic dowsing responses 15
    choosing a 14
physical body 44,45,50,56
place memory 68,69
power-centres 65,75,77-83

reflexology 50
repatterning 67,79
responses 19

signals, creating your own 15
sleep 26,75
smudging 69
sounds, healing and cleansing 69
space clearing 68-9
spine 44,46-9
spirit of the earth 56-9
spirituality 94,95
subtle body 44-5,56,66,70,83

tangible target dowsing 88
Traditional Chinese Medicine (TCM) 58
tuning-in 53
tutelary spirits 72-3,83

vitamins 26,28-9

water 25,26,27,69,86-7
wholeness 94-5
work 76-7

yin-yang 59,60,61,65,66,77,81

zones 50

Useful Addresses

Dr. Patrick MacManaway
Westbank Natural Health Centre
Strathmiglo
Fife, KY14 7QP
UK
Tel: 01337-868-945

Dr. Patrick MacManaway
Whole Earth Geomancy
4076 Shelburne Road, Suite 6
Shelburne
Vermont 05482
USA
Tel: 802-985-2266

British Society of Dowsers
Sycamore Barn
Tamley Lane
Hastingleigh
Ashford
Kent, TN2 5HW
Tel: 01233-750-253

American Society of Dowsers
Danville
Vermont 05828
Tel: 802-684-3417

The Dowsers Society of New South Wales
126 Fiddens Wharf Road
Killara
NSW 2071
Australia
Tel: 612 963 099 75

The Canadian Society of Dowsers
21 Oberon St.
Nepean
Ontario
K2H 7X6

Acknowledgements

I wish to acknowledge my grateful thanks to Rosanagh Bennet, Ann Preston, Dr Duncan Johnson and Dr Andrew Morrice for their expert advice and assistance in the areas of aromatherapy, reflexology, allergies, nutrition and flower remedies, and to acknowledge the contribution of the late Professor Cedric Wilson to the field of holistic research into allergies. Great thanks go to the project editors Debra Mayhew and Emma Gray for their gracious and patient guidance and support, and a wink and a nod and a bow both to Sig Lonegren for holding the flame and to my wife, Heather, for tending the fire.

    The publishers would like to thank the Chalice Well Trust in Glastonbury for their kind permission to allow photography in the Chalice Well Gardens. Thanks also to the following agencies for their kind permission to reproduce the pictures listed here: Fortean Picture Library: p12Tr. Gettyone Stone: pp11TR, 68BL, 81TR, 90TR. Science Photo Library: p45BL.
T=top, B=bottom, L=left, R=right.